This beautifully written work is a stunning breakthrough in the field of books on relationship. Its vision of direct, unmediated love could not be more original.

—Patricia Holt, former Book Review Editor,
San Francisco Chronicle

Undefended Love *is an invaluable resource for both identifying the major obstacles to intimacy and offering powerful modern and ancient tools for becoming undefended partners and our essential selves in all of our relationships.*

—Angeles Arrien, Ph.D., *The Four-Fold Way*
and *Signs of Life*

There is a new paradigm of relationship emerging from the shattered marriages of the past forty years. For the authors the key is a new kind of love, a love that is not burdened by the host of selves that are designed to keep us safe and separate from each other. Most of all, Undefended Love *is about a totally new kind of intimacy that is possible when one's heart is opened to the deeper possibilities of conscious relationship.*

—Hal and Sidra Stone, *Embracing Ourselves*
and *Embracing Each Other*

If intimacy is understood as stripping away your outer, more public ways of being and sharing your inner life with another, then Psaris and Lyons have written the definitive guidebook. Their description of the conditioned self and the journey to authenticity is not only precise and thorough, but extremely readable as well. For anyone on a journey to intimacy, this book will be a great delight to read.

—Susan Page, *How One of You Can Bring Two
of You Together* and *The 8 Essential Traits of
Couples Who Thrive*

Our deep and aching desire for enduring love drives many of us repeatedly into relationships that offer little chance of lasting fulfillment. In Undefended Love, *Psaris and Lyons go straight to the heart of what is most important to all of us: how to be in an intimate relationship that nourishes and sustains us and our partner.* Undefended Love *calls us to an expression of the courage and compassion needed to authentically know who we are and fearlessly share that truth with another person, to come home to ourselves, and experience the powerful joy of truly intimate loving. It is a jewel of a book.*

—Mary Manin Morrissey, *Building Your Field of Dreams*

UNDEFENDED
LOVE

JETT PSARIS, PH.D.

MARLENA S. LYONS, PH.D.

FOREWORD BY GAY AND KATHLYN HENDRICKS

NEW HARBINGER PUBLICATIONS, INC.

Publisher's Note

This publication is designed to provide accurate and authoritative information in regard to the subject matter covered. It is sold with the understanding that the publisher is not engaged in rendering psychological, financial, legal, or other professional services. If expert assistance or counseling is needed, the services of a competent professional should be sought.

Distributed in Canada by Raincoast Books.

Copyright © 2000 by Jett Psaris and Marlena S. Lyons
New Harbinger Publications, Inc.
5674 Shattuck Avenue
Oakland, CA 94609

The image on the cover is derived from a sculpture titled "The Dance of Love" by artist Never Chihumba.
Image courtesy of Zimbabwe Sculpture, Inc. (www.spiritsinstone.com)
Cover design by Poulson/Gluck Design
Edited by Jueli Gastwirth
Text design by Michele Waters

ISBN 1-57224-208-6 Paperback

New Harbinger Publications' Web site address: www.newharbinger.com

07   06   05

14   13   12   11   10   9   8

This book is lovingly dedicated to Gangaji.
Blessed one, our gratitude is eternal.

Intimacy—direct, unmediated, heart-to-heart connection with ourselves and with others—can only occur when the heart is *undefended*. To cut through our personal differences, to reach the unveiled part of ourselves that is deep enough to express the most profound and untamed aspects of our being means learning how to love and be loved without defenses and without obstructions. It means cultivating the capacity to be emotionally present even when we feel exposed or vulnerable; learning to relinquish the many strategies we have employed to feel safe and in control; and finding the courage to love without guarantees or requirements. Through developing the capacity for intimacy in this way, we discover love as an abiding presence in the emotional center of our being, our heart, and we can never again feel emotionally disconnected, incomplete, or unloved.

Contents

Foreword

Humans demand more from love every day. We want love to save us from loneliness, to make us happy, and to give us a purpose in life. We want love to make all the difficult decisions disappear. In short, we want love to do it all.

Human beings created romantic love—it's only been around for the last three hundred years or so—and have been loading it down with more baggage every day. Before the days of chivalry, there were alliances, there was property, there were bonds, and bonds broken, but there was no romance as we practice it. Today we are so inundated with images and hopes about love's promise that we can easily miss love's true purpose.

Also, humans love to be in love while secretly bad-mouthing love to ourselves and our friends. We want to be romantics, but the daily reality of "happily ever after" leaves a residue of cynicism on the rosiest cheeks. Most people we've surveyed assume that love doesn't last, that love disappoints, and that only compromise and settling for less have any possibility of success.

Jett Psaris and Marlena Lyons recognize that the modern love dance doesn't work. They have spent years helping people untangle themselves from the underbrush. *Undefended Love* clears the gnarled bramble of all our romantic illusions, a thorny patch that currently traps many of us, resulting in more than a 50 percent divorce rate.

In *Undefended Love*, Marlena and Jett unwind some of the most tangled beliefs that bedevil relationships, and the result will thrill and challenge you. You will find that they have made a home here in undefended love and have roamed the territory personally. They know that love's true purpose is to free the essential self.

Most of us hope that love will save us from "the worst thing" we can imagine about ourselves. For some, the worst thing is being alone. For others, the worst thing is being found worthless. Each of us hides this deepest wound from our partners and often from ourselves, while simultaneously craving love's absolution.

Undefended Love takes us right into the thicket of the worst thing, and it fairly skips along with the bone-deep certainty of knowing that true intimacy frees us. True intimacy utilizes fear and scythes through illusion to leave us, as Marlena and Jett have discovered, "at ease exactly as we are. We are at peace. We are peace itself."

In the twenty years that we have been collaborating to create relationships based in the essential self, we have heard one question more than any other. "How can I be myself and be fully with another?" *Undefended Love* describes the daily alchemy of essence that simple choices can create. Its ideas are simple, but not easy. For example, move toward your emotional discomfort rather than backpedaling away from it. Follow your experience to its source.

Why would any sane person choose to go into pain, to go into the unknown? Jett and Marlena know that freedom lies beyond understanding. They know that human beings want to be free more than they want to be safe. Freedom dances out beyond the reflex to defend. In *Undefended Love*, each page opens space unerringly and gives clear markers for the adventurous reader.

Imagine if you didn't have to defend yourself at all, ever. Imagine if your every interaction heralded discovery and more intimacy. Imagine that every day you could remember less and less and know more and more. *Undefended Love* makes the imagined real.

Gay and Kathlyn Hendricks
May, 2000

Personal Thanks

We'd like to thank the members of the Cutting Edge Group, Cultivating the Spiritual Warrior Within Group, Inner Work Group for Men, Inner Work Group for Women, and Living Truth Group where many of the concepts and methods contained in this book were refined. Your tireless dedication and courage to your healing and emotional liberation is an endless source of inspiration. Thanks also to all clients; students; and workshop, seminar, and retreat participants who have worked with us over the years. We thank you, we love you, and we are deeply honored you chose to share your personal journeys with us.

Rumi wrote: "Friend, our closeness is this: that wherever you put your foot, feel me in the firmness under you." Many friends selflessly gave of their time and energy to read and offer feedback at various stages of the manuscript's development. We felt the firmness of your support each time we lost our balance or faltered. Jenifer McKenna, Jennifer Welwood, Barbara Burdick-Zelnick, Gay and Kathlyn Hendricks, John Psaris, Terry Ryan, and David Schwartz. Thank you for your generosity and love.

A special debt of gratitude goes to Caroline Pincus, our book-midwife, who guided us through the search and selection of an agent, was an endless source of encouragement, and helped put finishing touches on the manuscript itself. We also wish to express our deep gratitude to our structural editor, Shoshana Alexander. She showed us how to give the manuscript a form and, to the extent that we have been able to follow her advice, she taught us how to write.

Others whom we would like to mention for their editorial contributions are Amanita Rosenbush, Priscilla Stucky, and Laura

Woodlief. Our thanks to Patrice Wynne, Suze Orman, Patricia Kelly, and Pat Holt who offered their expertise and advice when we needed it. Our deep appreciation, also, to the esteemed authors who gave of their time to read and endorse this project.

We would like to acknowledge our parents, John and Helene Psaris and T. George and Yolanda Khayat, and thank them for their love, care, and support. The more deeply we learn to love ourselves, the more grateful we are for the gift of their presence in our lives.

We see everyone and everything as our teacher; however, there are those to whom we are eternally indebted and who must be individually named: Jesus of Nazareth, Gautama Siddhartha, Sri Nisargadatta Maharaj, Sri Ramana Maharshi, Gangaji, Sri Aurobindo, H. W. L. Poonja, Jean Klein, J. Krishnamurti, Idries Shah, Hameed Ali, G. I. Gurdjieff, Chogyam Trungpa, Gay and Kathlyn Hendricks, John and Jennifer Welwood, Michelle Killoran, Anne Stine, Master Erica Stone, Jonathan Tenney, Patti Steurer, Ellyn Kaschak, Norman Egger, John Borghi, and Wiggsy Sivertsen.

Thanks go to our agent, Jim Levine, and the staff of James Levine Communications. Jim believed in the manuscript and worked tirelessly on our behalf, remaining steadfast in his resolve to publish this book well.

We would like to acknowledge our editor Jueli Gastwirth and the staff at New Harbinger Publications. Jueli's enthusiasm for the project was a spark that ignited a firestorm of commitment to undefended love—the book and the approach. We'd also like to thank our publisher Matt McKay, Kirk Johnson, Catharine Sutker, Kristin Beck, Amy Shoup, Dorothy Smyk, and Lauren Dockett, as well as those we have yet to meet at New Harbinger Publications.

Others helped in various ways, too many to name, but each deeply appreciated. You know who you are and we thank you for your contribution.

And finally, we would like to thank you the reader, without whom this work would be of little interest or value.

We shall not cease from exploration.
And the end of all our exploring
Will be to arrive where we started
And know the place for the first time.

—T. S. Eliot, *Four Quartets*

Introduction

When Anne first suggested that she and Tim consider deepening their commitment to each other, Tim responded with a resounding "no." He had recently gone through a heart-wrenching separation from the "love of his life." To him, relationship had come to mean failure—momentary highs followed by devastating lows, giving up what he wanted, emotional tugs-of-war, feeling trapped, dealing with conflict, and inevitable disappointment.

As he continued to describe what he "knew" relationship was about—everything he didn't want—Anne said, "If that's what it means to you, then I'm not interested either." That stopped him short. What was she talking about?

After a number of serious relationships, including a marriage lasting twelve years, Anne was ready to forge an entirely new manner of relating, one that surpassed anything she had experienced or seen. She wanted to create a union where her passion, warmth, generosity, and kindness toward her partner would grow over time, not falter and then be destroyed as had happened in her past. She was looking for a relationship that would be a vehicle, not a barrier, for self-discovery and mutual healing. For Anne, the only primary relationship worth having was one in which both parties work in a collaborative way, inviting and realizing their full potential individually and together.

What Anne was describing was a level of openheartedness and emotional honesty Tim had known in himself, but had only briefly been able to experience in relationship. Having failed to sustain this deep and unwavering connection—the experience of being united in heart and mind—with another, he had long ago given up on the possibility. As he listened to Anne, something within him began to shift. He intuitively knew that this was what he was seeking and that it was not only possible, it was what relationship was meant to be.

Intimacy and Undefended Love

When Anne and Tim first came to see us, they said they were seeking a deeper way of relating, one that surpassed conventional norms. They used the term "intimacy," but it did not take long to realize that by "intimacy" they did not mean sexuality per se. They wanted something deeper, something heart-based that could include sexuality as well as other avenues of expression.

They wanted to have a relationship that could not be shattered by the self-sabotaging influences rising from the emotional pain, frustrations, and setbacks in their pasts. They told us of their longing to know each other and to be known by each other—heart-to-heart, mind-to-mind, and body-to-body—without obstruction. They wanted to move beyond all perceived boundaries, to meet each other in a kind of nakedness, below the protective layers of habit and emotional reaction.

The further Anne and Tim delved into this exploration the more they realized the radical potential of this journey. If being emotionally intimate meant knowing and loving the very core of each other's being—with no buffer between them to obstruct or obscure the contact—they were committing themselves to becoming *undefended lovers.* On the one hand this felt like suicide, and on the other it felt wildly exciting.

Mapping the Terrain of the Undefended Heart

Lifelong patterns of defense are not easily released. To become undefended we have to recognize the complex ways we protect ourselves emotionally. We must use the unresolved hurts and losses from our pasts in a way that will expand, not limit, our ability to know and love one another.

In *Undefended Love* we will offer some powerful new tools for becoming undefended. We will first make the critical distinction between *personality*, which is actually a defense structure created to protect us from painful situations over which we had no control, and *essence*, the core of who we are. When our personalities become impenetrable and inflexible, they actually impede intimacy by imprisoning our hearts, the root of all intimate engagement. Over time, as we learn to lower our self-protective shields and experience the intensity and the exhilarating results of exposing ourselves in an undefended way, we learn to reside in our essence.

Essence is what is left after all defenses are stripped away; it is who we are when we are undefended. This unshakable center of being—a place where we feel loved, loving, whole, connected, and joyful—is the end to all experiences of emotional homelessness. It is the purpose of this book to help you get to essence, fully available to be loved and to love, without limitation, censorship, or restraint.

It may be helpful at this point to illustrate the difference between personality and essence a bit further, since they are, respectively, the starting point and final destination of the quest for intimate loving. Take a moment to imagine three figurines on a table in front of you. All are made of solid gold, each weighing 400 grams. One figurine is of a nun, another is a soldier, and the third is a mother cradling an infant. Each figurine is equal in terms of weight in gold. If we were to melt them down, we would receive the same amount of money for each 400 grams of gold, whether it had been cast as nun, soldier, or mother.

Consider which one of these figurines you would be most drawn to and why. Which one might you have little interest in or even dislike and why? Our reaction to these shapes is a function of our personality. What we are attracted to or repelled by in each figure depends on the associations we carry from our past. We end up responding to our prior associations with that image rather than to the pure gold of which each is made.

H. W. L. Poonja (1992), an eminent teacher and holy man who lived in India until his death in 1997, offered the above metaphor as a way to understand the difference between our essence and the personality we so often mistake for who we are. Like pure gold cast into different forms, each of us is fundamentally good, valuable, and whole. However, when we get lost in identifying ourselves and others by our personalities, we are left relating through a complex latticework of past associations: Only our personalities meet, leaving our hearts untouched.

To achieve the naked, passionate, and meaningful contact that results in intimacy, we must face our deepest fears about emotional survival. Permanently closing the gap between us means removing all barriers, all of the ways we have learned to shield ourselves emotionally, thus exposing us—undefended and defenseless—to each other. But as we begin to experience our essence, we also begin to understand the profound implications of this journey: We see the extent to which our personalities have been obstructing our ability to experience ourselves and one another directly, and the limitless joy to be had when we love without barriers.

Reaching Common Ground

Many popular books on relationship suggest that the way to make relationship work is through understanding the "differences" between us. It is easier to attribute relationship friction, tension, and distance to difference, to something beyond our control. If we believe that our partner is an alien from another planet because he or she is a member of the opposite sex, we do not have to investigate or struggle to surpass our conditioning. But, we contend, it is precisely this social conditioning, and not actual difference, that gets in the way of intimate, heart-to-heart connection.

Many women believe that there is little potential for undefended intimacy in their relationships with men. Often they rely on women friends for that depth of connection, thus further reducing the likelihood of meaning and satisfaction in their primary relationships. In our work with hundreds of clients—individuals, couples, and groups—we have found that the *intrinsic capacity* for intimacy is the same in women and men, that men are just as willing and capable as women of moving through their defenses. Gender conditioning can delay this inclination in men, but once they recognize this and experience intimacy, the work of identifying and dissolving their defense structures is exactly the same as it is for women. We have also found no appreciable difference between how straight and gay partners do this work. The content of the conditioning might differ, but even this material is not as diverse as one would initially expect.

Intimacy is experienced when we relate from the *gold* of who we are. Emotionally intimate couples are committed to digging below experiences of opposition and difference until they strike gold. By viewing all differences, even male and female, as two different castings of the same gold, and our "gender-conditioning" (in this particular example) as stains obscuring its brightness, each of us can engage in the challenging work of cleaning and polishing ourselves to bring out the gold from under the dust and grime.

In the course of striving to expose this golden core—our common ground—we become more available to one another and we feel increasingly intimate. The more intimate we become, the less alienating are our differences and the less emotional distance we experience when these differences do emerge.

Even if only one person in a relationship is committed to true intimacy, he or she can begin opening up something valuable in the partnership. Our work as individuals creates a ripple effect that can transform our primary partner, our family, even our friends and community. The more unleashed and unhindered by the weight of social and personal conditioning we become, the more our loved ones will want to join us. The feeling of freedom and possibility is contagious.

The desire for undefended love is fueling a radical shift in the way couples come together and stay together. Instead of becoming involved primarily through sexual chemistry, psychological and spiritual orientation are playing ever larger roles. As Ted, a man who describes himself as a "regular guy," told us six months into a new relationship: "You'll never believe it—we haven't had sex yet. We laugh and we talk about everything. I love being with her. I want to tell her things I've never told anyone before. The way we are together feels like how I used to feel *after* having sex—openhearted and easy. When we do decide to be sexual, I can see that it will be just one more way to enjoy each other—not the only way—which is what sex has been for me in the past."

Loving Irreversibly

The journey to the heart of intimacy is not always easy. It requires a heart full of courage and, sometimes, it demands all we've got to give. The end of the journey, however, promises an enhanced capacity to experience an ongoing state of joy and peace undisturbed by the intermittent bouts of emotional pain, loss, and other challenging feelings that emerge in the course of one's life. Whether the ability to be undefended is realized spontaneously through good fortune, or over time through vigilant self-examination, the journey is worth every step (and leap) along the way. Undefended love is a *developed capacity* available to everyone.

We need only two things on this journey: a map of the terrain and a sincere commitment to use relationship as the vehicle to open our hearts and express our full potential. The map is contained in these pages and we trust it has found its way into the hands and hearts of eager cojourniers.

In the movie *Harvest of Fire* (1996), the protagonist says, "When two lives touch they can never again be completely separated." This is the potential of undefended intimacy—to touch deeply and irreversibly. It is an alchemical process in which each of us is transformed. The result is a deeper capacity to love from the profound and unshakable recognition of our golden core.

May you find a way of life and of loving that is all you've dreamed.

Jett Psaris and Marlena S. Lyons
Oakland, California
May, 2000

CHAPTER 1

A Flame in Our Hearts: The Longing for Intimacy

Our sense of urgency to have relationships that feel intimate is often frustrated by a lack of understanding about what intimacy is, how to achieve it, and why it cannot be sustained. Intimacy is difficult to define and widely misunderstood. To explore its true meaning, we have to move beyond conventional definitions and challenge what we believe to be true. Many of us think of intimacy as having sex, being physically or emotionally close, or exchanging deeply held confidences. But if specific behaviors such as these produce intimacy, then why don't we experience intimacy each time we do them? What makes one sexual encounter intimate and another not? If cultivating closeness is an avenue to intimacy, why do so many couples who have attained it report flatness, boredom, loss of vitality, or a sense of being "stuck" rather than feeling passionately alive in each other's presence? If confiding in another is supposed to bring about intimacy, why does one communication make us flush to our roots while another leaves us untouched and unmoved?

Behaviors are not the source of our intimate experiences. That is why the use of the term *intimacy* as a euphemism for being sexual is so misleading. Although some of us have experienced true intimacy and union through sex, *what is intimate is not the behavior itself but the state of being we reach within ourselves and with our partners.*

We all know what it feels like to experience a deeper part of ourselves, outside our daily routines and superficial exchanges. It is this feeling that we reclaim during moments of profound connection with another—a deep experience of ourselves. This is the key to intimacy: our ability to dive below the familiar world of our "outer self" into the less understood provenance of our human potential.

The Heart of Intimacy

The word intimacy comes from the Latin word *intimus,* which means "pertaining to one's deepest nature," that which is "innermost and essential." This essence lies well below the roles and obligations we have assumed in our daily lives. Experiencing this essential aspect of ourselves and of our partners is the source of true intimacy. It may be the outcome of a sexual encounter or any of the other behaviors we link to intimacy, but it is not limited to or defined by them.

As we deepen our ability to contact and respond from this core of our being we discover connection with everything around us. At some point, most of us have experienced this feeling of being fully alive and awake while also connected to the larger web of life. These moments often occur spontaneously while in nature, which is why it feels so right to go to neighborhood parks, the mountains, or the ocean when we are troubled or trying to reconnect with ourselves. In the words of poet Izumi Shikibu (1990):

> Watching the moon
> at midnight,
> solitary, mid-sky,
> I knew myself completely,
> no part left out.

Walking in the silence of an ancient grove of redwood trees, gazing at the majesty of a starry sky, or witnessing another day washed away in a blood-red sunset can bring us into closer relationship with our essential nature and our place in the world.

Spiritual practices such as meditation, prayer, or yoga deepen our capacity to feel and sustain this fullness of connection to ourselves and to life. Through these pursuits we gain confidence that we can know the part of us that is loving and peaceful, and we learn to trust that those qualities abide within us, even when they are not accessible. These practices help us quiet our minds and open our hearts, making us less susceptible to the emotional and circumstantial tides of our daily lives.

But what happens when we try to bring this deep and peaceful aspect of ourselves into relationship with another? It is certainly easier to feel self-assured, peaceful, and centered while looking at the ocean, chanting a mantra, listening to music, or sitting beneath a majestic oak than when we are in the presence of a significant other. To be so open and available to another requires being vulnerable and unguarded. In those rare moments when we do meet heart-to-heart, emotionally and psychologically naked, we feel exhilarated and awake to a degree we seldom experience anywhere else in our lives.

Whether we have experienced this possibility with someone through falling in love or through an exquisitely vulnerable sexual encounter, at these times when our defenses are stripped away by the power and immediacy of the present moment, we feel known and loved—accurately and fully. These experiences stand out above all others, becoming the gold standard for feeling connected, cared for, and cherished. We then mistakenly attribute the immeasurable celebration this elicits in us to the way we experienced this opening, instead of understanding it as a reflection of our natural state when our hearts are undefended and available. We try over and over to recapture this sense of ourselves through sexuality and falling in love—only to find each brief experience of connection giving way to some familiar sense of emotional distance and separation.

The Central Dilemma

Many people have absorbed something of the cultural belief that if we find the right partner and love each other enough, the outcome will be the passionate yet secure relationship we have always hoped for. When we don't achieve this, as is so often the case, we believe something is wrong with the relationship, with us, or with our partners. In desperate attempts to fix the situation, we try to become what our partners want, or to get our partners to change, so that we can enjoy what relationship "is supposed to be."

Jean and Greg: Applying the Undefended Approach

Jean and her husband, Greg, both in their mid-forties, attended one of our weekend retreats. As they introduced themselves, they explained that in the beginning of their marriage, each believed their "other half" had been found. "I kept telling my friends that I had 'lucked out' and found my true love," Greg began. Jean added, "Greg used to call me his soul mate." They were sexually compatible, shared common interests, and enjoyed each other's company immensely. Now, however, after four years of marriage they were contemplating separation. They had come to the retreat to get away from home, think things over, and try to come to terms with what had gone wrong. "At the minimum," Jean told us, "I want to know what happened so I don't repeat the same mistakes next time—if there is a next time."

When Jean and Greg volunteered to work in front of the group on the first day of the retreat, Jean began by saying that she knew Greg loved her, but she did not feel that he was still "in love" with her. "His eyes don't go soft as he watches me across the room anymore. I miss the way he used to pull me down onto his lap for a moment's closeness before we would both rush off to work. He doesn't phone me during the day, and he comes home later at night."

When it was Greg's turn to speak, he told the group he felt unhappy, trapped, and restless. "A year or so ago the relationship began to feel routine: television after work, errands on the weekends, and not much in between." He added that their sexual relationship, which had been exciting when they were first together, had begun to feel predictable.

Some couples, like Jean and Greg, briefly achieve the societal vision of a "perfect" relationship—only to find it ending in dissatisfaction. They come to our retreats and workshops lamenting: "The spark is missing." "We've grown apart." "All the passion is gone." "I look at him and I no longer see the person I married." They have a deep yearning that they imagine can only be fulfilled by returning things to the way they were in the beginning of their relationship.

Here's what Jean and Greg didn't realize: The glow we experience in the first stage of relationship is a *promise* of the possibility of being deeply known. The seeds of intimate connection planted at the beginning will blossom only after we free ourselves from the defense structures that inevitably surface, threatening our bliss.

A participant at the retreat asked Jean how she reacted to the increasing distance between them. "The more I felt Greg pulling away from me, the harder I worked to win him back," Jean replied. "I turned myself inside out trying to be the person I thought he wanted me to be." The more she focused on changing herself, the more depleted and resentful she became. Meanwhile, Greg blamed Jean for the boredom he was experiencing. He began to spend more time drinking with colleagues and fantasizing about "breaking loose" from the marriage and being with someone new.

We enter relationship hoping and believing that the expansive and delightful stage will continue on its own, unimpeded by the automatic, repetitive patterns that will inevitably emerge from the unfinished emotional business of our past. When the all-too-familiar habits do surface and the initial openness dissolves, we feel betrayed by our partners. If this happens in relationship after relationship, we eventually conclude that such deep connections are not sustainable. Our longing for genuine intimacy becomes entwined with the expectation of disappointment and pain. The resulting tension between hope that intimacy is possible and hopelessness that we may never achieve it, or cannot sustain it, leaves us alternately reaching out for and guarding against undefended contact.

Our defenses may give us the feeling of protection, but they also keep us from experiencing the intimacy we desire. This, then, is the central dilemma in which we find ourselves: We long to surpass our routine, passionless, or conflict-driven relationships, but we are afraid to take the personal risks necessary to break free from our old, self-protective ways of being. Instead, we choose to stay emotionally safe, comfortable, and in control. Once we recognize that all our efforts to change our partner's behavior, or to find a "better" partner, have failed to provide us with what we most desire in relationship, only then do we begin the challenging *self*-exploration that is necessary for a deep and nourishing connection with another.

In the process of learning to tolerate our fears, interrupt old defensive patterns, and let go of our attempts to manipulate our partners, we focus our attention on increasing our awareness of deeper layers of our experience. Finding intimacy begins with discovering ourselves, not with fixing or controlling ourselves or our partners. We have to be visible before we can be seen. We have to be available before our hearts can be affected. And we have to be present before we can be intimate. When we can drop all pretenses and relate with a heart that is undefended, we can finally discover the unmistakable connection we long to have with our authentic selves and with our partners.

Greg, in the course of his self-exploration, realized that the experience he was having with Jean had been repeated in his two prior marriages. In each, he unconsciously made it his partner's responsibility to keep him happy. "When the excitement of the early stages of our relationship wore off, I found myself back in an all-too-familiar place. It seems that no matter who I get involved with, within a few years I end up unhappy for the same vague reasons." Greg acknowledged that as long as his happiness was reliant on someone else, he was always at risk of being dissatisfied. It was now his job, he realized, to learn more about his discontent instead of trying to distract himself from it.

After a great deal of introspection and self-confrontation during the weekend retreat, Jean realized what the current state of her marriage was demanding from her: "There is an absence of me in my life. I'm what's missing in this relationship." Jean had organized her life around Greg—what he liked and didn't like, what he wanted and didn't want, his beliefs and his convictions. "Although I'd like to say that I did this out of my love for him, that is only partly true. I now realize that I focused my attention on Greg because I was too afraid to face the emptiness inside me." As if trying to grasp hold of her heart, Jean clutched at her chest as she admitted, "I'm afraid that there is no me in here."

When we experience conflict or dissatisfaction in our relationships, we are being called on to develop something in ourselves that is weak, hidden, or unknown. Rather than leave Greg, as she had been on the verge of doing only a few days before, Jean now wanted to create a relationship that reflected two whole people. This meant that she must learn more about her inner life, even if for a time the only thing she found there was emptiness, in the hope that she would begin to experience an authentic identity, one belonging to her, not superimposed on her.

We will only attain the perfection we seek in relationship when we learn to relinquish our vision of the "perfect couple" and forge a union that is completely authentic to the individuals involved. When connection with the "other" seems all but impossible, we stand on a precipice: Will we embark on a personal quest for a deeper understanding, or will we retreat into the safety of our belief systems, which tell us that if a relationship is right, the good times will continue? When we allow each dilemma to shake our view of the world until we no longer know what is "right," we activate our longing for authenticity and belonging, and set foot on the path to undefended love.

The Dual Yearning of the Human Heart

Many seekers arrive at our seminars and retreats filled with a restless yearning. For some the yearning may be a tiny ember kept alive through the haunting memory of what it felt like to fall in love. For others it may be a vague sense that there must be more to life, love, and connection than they are currently experiencing. They long to feel loved, to love another without reservation, or to deepen an already satisfying relationship. The longing is sometimes expressed as a desire for certainty and clarity, and the wish for the confidence to express themselves more creatively in the world.

Those who have chronically suppressed their yearning come to these retreats saying their lives are characterized by a flatness or boredom they can't seem to move beyond. Some are not quite able to name what they yearn for, but they come feeling compelled to seek it. A woman who attended one of our seminars on her eighty-first birthday resolutely proclaimed, "There is a flame burning in my heart and it will not be denied." In our work we call this flame the *dual yearning of the human heart*.

On the one hand, we yearn for an increased sense of connection with another. This basic human desire has not changed much over the centuries. In an often-quoted biblical passage that expresses the fullness of human love, Ruth says to Naomi: "Wherever you go, I will go. Wherever you lodge, I will lodge. Your people shall be my people. Where you die, I will die; and there I will be buried" (Ruth 1:16, 17). In our own lives this yearning is often experienced as the desire for closeness with another. We long to be partnered, to feel welcomed, to belong, to know our "other half" or "twin flame."

On the other hand, we have a personal desire to experience and connect deeply with ourselves. Often this begins with wondering what our fundamental nature is, the part of us below what is expected of us socially and personally. We long to know our source in a direct way, a heightened self-awareness that brings with it a sense of vitality and personal authority. When we are truthful with ourselves, we can meet life face-to-face, unrehearsed, immersing ourselves fully in every experience.

A pull exists within each of us to satisfy this dual yearning of the human heart. We can trust that yearning as a call to journey to the heart of intimacy, whether through the search for a deeper connection with another or a desire to connect more deeply with ourselves. We long to love from the fullness of our undefended hearts and we long to be loved unconditionally and without reservation. This flame in our hearts will guide us as unwaveringly as the force that guides salmon on their journey halfway around the world to battle their way upstream to their point of origin. Like them, we have a destiny to return home, to be fully "at home" within ourselves as well as deeply "at home" with another.

Our Destiny to Return "Home"

Home. By simply saying the word aloud or silently cradling it in our hearts, for a moment we may feel still, complete, and free. Where is our true home? The great mistake we make is believing that we can find it "out there," in a partner, in a place, or by fulfilling an endless stream of desires. Although it is true that the feeling of home can be *evoked* by something "out there," such as a lover, cherished pet, child, or idyllic pastoral setting, home can only be reached and sustained through connecting with something "in here," deep inside each of us.

Embarking on the quest for undefended intimacy is setting out for home. It is the path to wholeness, love, and joy, in ourselves and with another. In time we discover that we were home all along; we just didn't know it. When we grasp this truth, we realize that despite passing experiences of emotional distress, impasses in relationship, or times when we are embroiled in defensiveness, we retain the capacity to feel complete, full, open, and at peace. We are no longer thrown off balance by life's circumstances when rooted with certainty and confidence in our "place at the table." Only then can we open our hearts fully.

The dual yearning of the human heart finds its satisfaction in the struggle to know ourselves at our most vulnerable levels. *The deeper we know ourselves, the deeper is our capacity to know others intimately.* "Loving does not at first mean merging, surrendering, and uniting with another person," poet Rainer Maria Rilke writes in *Letters to a Young Poet* (1954). "It is a high inducement for the individual to ripen, to become something in himself . . . it is a great, demanding claim on him, something that chooses him and calls him to vast distances." It is our deep hunger for this level of loving that moves us beyond our resistance, fear, and shortcomings to see what is special and unique about us. It allows us to see the profound core of another and to have that core be fully seen in ourselves.

Choosing to Follow the Flame

To reach the unveiled part of ourselves that is deep enough to express the most profound and untamed aspects of our being means learning how to love and be loved without defenses and without obstructions. It means cultivating the capacity to be emotionally present even when we feel exposed or vulnerable; learning to relinquish the many strategies we have employed to feel safe and in control; and finding the courage to love without guarantees or requirements. Through developing the capacity for intimacy in this way, we discover love as an abiding presence in the emotional center of our being, our heart, and from that moment on, we will never again feel emotionally disconnected, incomplete, or unloved.

Most of us have defended and protected ourselves for so many years we have lost direct access to our hearts; we do not know how to love in an unguarded way. We keep waiting for the right circumstances, the right partner, the right moment to be vulnerable. We may go on waiting endlessly, missing the very opportunity before us.

An Exemplary Commitment: Applying the Undefended Approach

Sitting in an airport lounge, waiting for a flight on the way to a conference outside of Boston, we found ourselves drawn into the last few minutes of a television program. The host was beginning to interview a couple we found immediately intriguing. Despite a marked contrast in physical appearance—his muscular build suggested a life of hard physical labor while she was small, thin, and somewhat fragile—they revealed a remarkable harmony in their movements and tone. While speaking, each often turned toward the other, offering small gestures of love and encouragement.

She began by relating that their relationship had been on-again, off-again over a period of five years. He explained the reason: In the early stages of the relationship he was "commitment phobic." She continued: Because he was not willing to commit to a long-term partnership, she broke off the relationship to search for someone who would. Soon after, she started dating another man. Unbeknownst to her, he was HIV positive, with the beginning symptoms of AIDS. She discovered his secret only after she contracted AIDS herself.

At this point in the interview they both fell silent for several moments. Slowly and thoughtfully, he picked up where she had left off. "When I heard what had happened, I came back into her life and asked her to marry me." When the interviewer asked him why, his unequivocal reply was that he realized how deeply he loved her and that he would have very little time to be with her now that she had contracted the disease. Although perhaps there was a part of him that initially may have felt safe in a "long-term commitment" that had a short-term end in sight, the urgency of the situation opened his heart, enabling him to give himself fully to love.

"Compliments of this dreadful disease, I learned quickly to put aside all of my usual defenses," he said. "I no longer have the luxury to act out my old patterns, because every moment with her is too precious and too limited." Although our flight was announced, we lingered a moment to hear this man's parting advice: If you want to see what's possible, how you can love another without reservation, all you have to do is imagine that your partner has contracted a deadly disease and you have only six months left together. What kind of person do you want to be in the remaining time you have with one another?

The Fire of Our Internal Struggle

We can consciously choose to love in an undefended way without waiting for life to orchestrate a circumstance that compels us to do so. This does not mean artificially changing behavior, suppressing uncomfortable emotions, or pretending problems don't exist. We cannot bypass or transcend what lies within and between us. But inquiring into how we might feel if we had very little time left with one another can shift us off our "position." We can recognize that life gives us a choice: Defend against and reject our experience or accept our vulnerability and let it be a source of guidance. Only when we can relax the rigidity we feel in relation to another can we discover our intrinsic strength and find the common ground between us.

When we simply remain present in the midst of our dilemma, the fire of our internal struggles softens our hard places and sharp ens our insight. Our dedication to love with an unguarded heart offers us the opportunity to use problems in our relationships as avenues to the core of our being. "When you have an issue in your life," author and self-realization teacher A. H. Almaas (1987) instructs, "the point is not . . . just to resolve the issue; the point is to grow through resolving it." The journey toward undefended intimacy refines our personality and opens us to a larger perception of our gifts and inner resources. When challenged, our unconscious belief of "I can't" gives way to an experience of "I can." When we tenaciously endure our feelings of loneliness and isolation—without seeking escape or distraction—we discover connection everywhere. When we recognize our deep and abiding belief that our being is inadequate or flawed, we realize the larger self within which these limited views are contained. The intimacy we seek is a capacity gained through our struggle to stretch beyond the person we have known ourselves to be.

Cultivating the personal depth and maturity necessary to live an intimate life is a developmental task facing each and every one of us. It is not an easy one, but in terms of relationship, it creates a sense of belonging, clarity, and joy that can never be taken away. It requires a heart that is strong enough to let some of our usual guards down so we can touch and be touched by another. It demands that we interrupt our emotional reactions when lashing out seems beyond our control. It calls on us to struggle against every instinct that compels us to attack, shield ourselves, or hide.

The dedication to stay open and present in the face of fear comes naturally when we are in contact with our deepest sense of well-being. When we begin by nourishing and cultivating the root of our being, everything else follows. "Fruit falls from a tree naturally when ripe," author and meditation teacher Jack Kornfield (1993) lovingly reminds us. The emotional maturity that enables us to live in a truly intimate relationship unfolds as we cultivate intimacy with our own deepest nature, our essence.

Taking on the First Task

Viktor Frankl (1984), the renowned psychologist who found meaning in life even in a Nazi concentration camp, drops us straight to the bottom line with his statement: "When we are no longer able to change a situation, we are challenged to change ourselves." The potential for intimacy will be realized by those who see that despite the stream of significant others passing through a revolving door of relationships, their own preoccupations seem always to interfere with sustaining deep levels of connection.

There is one non-negotiable ticket for admission to creating and sustaining intimate partnerships: the understanding that what we are experiencing in relationship is a reflection of our own internal state of being. This means inquiring into each thought, feeling, and behavior with the recognition that our emotional reactions can best tell us something about ourselves, rather than about our partners. The supreme principle in developing the capacity to live and love with an undefended heart is this: Challenge and liberate yourself from your own defensiveness before you try to critique and evaluate the behaviors and reactions of others.

This is not to suggest that what is emerging has nothing to do with our partners. But focusing our attention on others can too readily lead to that old familiar slippery slope of accusations and counter-accusations. Usually an issue or conflict has something in it of value for both partners. Our complaint about or evaluation of our partner may be true anywhere from 1 percent to 100 percent, but even if we are 100 percent correct, all we get out of this is being right. This does not address and heal what prompted our reaction to our partner's behavior.

When our stance remains unexamined, we don't deepen and we don't grow. We always suggest to clients that they use their reactions as fuel to dismantle the defense their emotionality is keeping in place before attempting to hold their partners accountable. The details of how this is accomplished are the subject of chapters 6 through 10.

When working with a couple for the first time, we ask if they are willing to challenge their personal view of reality and their defensive reactions as part of discovering a deeper truth about themselves and each other. Usually both partners affirm their commitment to do "whatever it takes." The real test of their readiness comes when they move their attention from each other—usually in the form of blame—to an examination of their own behavior and reactions.

Stacey and Hal: Applying the Undefended Approach

Stacey and Hal were deadlocked over ways to continue their relationship. Every time Stacey felt threatened, she simply left— emotionally and physically. Hal felt devastated by this behavior. After hearing from each of them in a joint session, we turned to Hal to ask him to explore his reaction. We could see that Hal felt put on the spot. "Why are you focusing on *my* behavior?" Hal asked. "Stacey is the one who shuts me out and doesn't tell me what's going on!" We assured him that we would investigate whatever was motivating Stacey's behavior shortly. Before we did that, however, would Hal be willing to identify what he felt when Stacey withdrew?

Hal told us he felt we were telling him that he was doing something wrong. "So it's important that you are not wrong. What do you know about that?" we asked him. "What is your experience when someone says that you are doing something wrong? Can you describe what that feeling brings up for you?" Hal still could not turn his attention inward. "I feel like you are implying that I am wrong to feel the way I feel when she leaves," he went on. We asked,

"How do *you* feel when she leaves? Where do *you* go when she leaves?" At this point an exasperated Hal exclaimed, "What's the difference how *I* feel? *She's* the one who withdraws and that's what's wrong here!"

Not surprisingly, Stacey was solidly entrenched in her position that Hal was the problem. "Well, I'm glad you get to see what I'm dealing with. His constant need for attention is driving me nuts. I want him to back off."

Mutually unwilling to explore their own contribution to this ingrained dynamic, they remained desperately attached to their sincere belief that if the other changed, the problems of their relationship would be solved. As long as Hal and Stacey continued focusing on each other's behaviors, they avoided facing the unbearable feelings that rose in them when the other played out the familiar pattern of anger and withdrawal.

We've probably learned many times over that confronting or trying to change our partner's behavior never results in a lasting resolution. Only when we resist blaming our partner and attend to the experience we are having within ourselves can we begin to investigate what is stimulating our emotionally charged reactions. The response that would promise more than a temporary break in Stacey and Hal's impasse would be for them to focus on their own sensitivity to the other's behavior.

As we will see, problems in relationship cut so deeply that we can't help but respond protectively, wanting our partner to stop the behavior we feel is "causing" the problem. But if, using the problem as a starting point, we allow ourselves to challenge why we are having the emotional reaction, we can begin to permanently transform these patterns of interaction. For example, if our partner consistently withdraws, and we are committed to cultivating intimacy, we must discover the deep abyss of loneliness and rage that is evoked in us by this behavior rather than list all the friends who support our view that our partner is emotionally unavailable. The capacity for undefended intimacy unfolds when we have developed the ability to confront, investigate, and transform our own behavior patterns and beliefs, regardless of what we feel our partner is doing to "push our buttons."

Certainly this is not an excuse to stay in a relationship that is abusive. You don't have to continue suffering abuse in order to examine the underlying issues that got you there. The path outlined in these pages is meant for those committed to loving themselves and their partners with an open, undefended heart. Assuming you have ascertained, with the help of a professional (if there is any doubt whatsoever), that you are not in an abusive relationship, you may discover a pattern of feeling abused if, for instance, your partner has a different perspective from yours. Or, your extreme sensitivity to "being made wrong" may result in believing that your partner is emotionally destructive when he or she is simply pointing out a difference in experience. Whether you choose to stay or leave, your capacity to love without defenses will unfold only as you probe your own reactions and make their transformation your first priority.

Over time, Stacey and Hal learned to use their discomfort as a way of uncovering the vulnerabilities hidden below their conviction that they were right. As a result, they discovered much more about themselves and each other than they would have by continuing to blame one another for their own pain and discomfort. The deeper we know that "as without, so within," the greater are our chances of recognizing and navigating our way through the parts of us that are not fully conscious and that block us from knowing ourselves as the intrinsically whole, loving, and strong individuals we are.

When our commitment to knowing and revealing ourselves is greater than the need to hide, protect, or defend—or to blame others—we pull on a thread that promises to unravel all the layers of protection that keep us isolated and disconnected. Dissolving the barriers of self-defense is the first task on the path to fulfilling our longing to live with an undefended heart.

It Is Possible

Profoundly meaningful and sustainable connection is possible. It begins with recognizing that the distress and dissatisfaction we experience in our relationships are absolutely necessary to achieving the intimacy we desire. Some Native Americans would call the challenges we encounter in relationship "good medicine," intended to make us whole again. If we see all our interactions with our partners as good medicine, then, when we feel uncomfortable, we have a bigger context in which to view our responses. We can see that the challenges are there to support us in learning to realize our full potential as emotionally mature adults, capable of profoundly loving ourselves and each other without conditions or restrictions.

When we welcome our difficulties, we allow the power of our love to guide us to unexpected sources of strength and courage beneath our pain and reactivity. This enables us to do the necessary work of facing the dark relics of our past. We can harness the inevitable emotional pain and discomfort that is stimulated in relationship and place them in the service of forging an unwavering love for ourselves and our partners.

When we allow ourselves to be known and loved for our essential openness, which can feel both vulnerable and exhilarating, and choose to know and love another, totally and without reservation, we arrive at the heart of intimacy. We may embark on the journey burdened by past disappointments and fearing yet another failure, but we can trust the dual yearning of our heart. It will lead us beyond our current limits and defenses until we eventually know ourselves and another at our most vulnerable and authentic levels.

Ultimately, intimacy is about the freedom to be ourselves. True emotional freedom means no longer needing confirmation, agreement, or validation from another to know our basic goodness. Knowing our intrinsic worth, we are able to be present with ourselves and our partners, whatever the circumstances. This freedom means no longer being defined by our personal history. It means being who we are essentially, unencumbered, and undefended. Jennifer Welwood (1998), our dear friend and a gifted therapist and poet, affirms that the journey requires that we are unconditionally willing to face what we fear most.

> Willing to experience aloneness,
> I discover connection everywhere;
> Turning to face my fear,
> I meet the warrior who lives within;
> Opening to my loss,
> I gain the embrace of the universe;
> Surrendering into emptiness,
> I find fullness without end.
> Each condition I flee from pursues me,
> Each condition I welcome transforms me
> and becomes itself transformed
> Into its radiant, jewel-like essence.

I bow to the one who has made it so,
Who has crafted this Master Game;
To play it is purest delight—
To honor its form true devotion.

When we open our hearts to the wonder of the journey and search through the pain for the truth of our experience, we begin to glimpse a new light that will guide us deeper into ourselves, below our insecurities and the broken dreams of our lives. There we will meet our whole, undamaged, and pristine essential self. In touch with this essential self, we can experience powerful levels of intimacy while engaged in the most ordinary behaviors. This is the promise of undefended intimacy. This is the satisfaction of the longing to love and be loved, directly, immediately, and without restriction.

CHAPTER 2

The Essential Self: The Heart of Who We Are

Intentionally choosing to love in an intimate way—rather than waiting for circumstances to bring us moments of spontaneous intimacy—requires learning to open to our heart of hearts, the treasure at the core of our being, our essence. In this core place of fullness and goodness, we are without fear; we are connected to everyone and everything; we feel awake, vital, and alive. Seated in this center of our unconditioned self, we perceive the exquisite beauty and richness of human love with such poignancy that more typical expressions of connection feel pale and lifeless in comparison.

Many of us spend our lives entirely unaware of our essence. We consider ourselves to be the compilation of thoughts, behaviors, habits, reactions, and conditioned patterns that make up our personalities; but, beneath that identity an unrealized human potential lies dormant. This abiding presence deep within us is not something we can perceive with our intellect, emotions, or senses. But we can directly know its substance and power. We begin by opening to the possibility—perhaps initially through our intellect—that there is more to us than we experience on a daily basis. We do not have to understand our essence or be able to express it: Simply keeping in mind that a world of riches lies within invites this reality into our conscious mind.

We have all experienced our essence, alone or with another. Such experiences had a powerful impact on our personal lives. They remain unforgettable because we experienced ourselves as more awake than usual, energized, open, expansive, connected, and vital. These were moments when life orchestrated a stopping point that brought us to the immediacy and power of the present. They might include:

- Falling in love

- A time in nature

- A time when you felt treasured and valued by another

- A time when you felt a deep appreciation for another

- Being present at a birth or giving birth

- Saying good-bye to loved ones or cherished pets prior to their deaths

At these moments our essential self shone through in the qualities we felt and exhibited. Because connecting with our personal essence is so powerful, however, we often misunderstand its source. We believe that it is the specific circumstance or occasion that causes us to feel a certain way. This is particularly true when we fall in love and believe our partner makes us feel joyful, alive, enthusiastic, etc. Such a dangerous misunderstanding keeps us from recognizing that these qualities are intrinsic to us. Someone with whom we are falling in love or an enlightened teacher may help us experience these qualities more readily, but they are the pure, basic aspects of our essential self. Circumstances or individuals may evoke them, but these treasures dwell within us permanently.

What Is Essence?

According to *The American Heritage Dictionary*, *essence* means: "The intrinsic or indispensable properties that serve to characterize or identify something; the inherent, unchanging nature of a thing." Our essence, then, is our innate, defining substance. It is not the person we have learned to be or have been conditioned to believe we are, not our personality, but the most authentic part of us, in the most distilled form. It is elemental. Like a prime number, it cannot be broken down into component parts. Our essence is concentrated and pure, like the nectar that remains after the excess liquid of a fruit juice has been boiled away.

This pristine level of being can most easily be seen in babies and in those who have attained spiritual enlightenment. In both, there is an uninhibited, undistracted attention to the moment. Our friend's eight-month-old son Dominic awakens us to this possibility over and over. While our caring attention and guidance makes his parents appear to be the givers, Dominic's innocent presence is a gift he offers us every day.

Like most babies, Dominic's divine nature is so visible and unobstructed that he lights up the world without doing a thing. His face is bright and expansive like a cloudless sky. Delight ripples so entirely through his body that a smile on his lips completes itself in the kicking of his tiny feet. He expresses his sheer joy in life by thrusting both hands wildly into the air. Very little obstructs the spontaneous, ecstatic openness of his essence. Dominic brings home the truth of the words of Jesus of Nazareth, "You are the light of the world."

Although there is a difference in the way these qualities are expressed in a baby as opposed to a mature, enlightened adult, in both we perceive the same openness, spontaneity, and awakened presence, so unlike the human norm. And while each teacher and enlightened master emanates a different quality of essence, they all share one thing—they exemplify what it means to be a free human being. Inspired by the visible radiance of one such teacher, a good friend remarked, "The sun becomes a moon compared with this brightness." This potent luminosity, inherent in every one of us, is brilliant beyond all manifest creation. This is why coming into contact with a being in whom essence is fully manifest is so transforming.

The first time I (Jett) came face-to-face with Gangaji, a spiritual teacher in the Hindu Advaita Vedanta tradition, and looked into her eyes, I felt pierced straight through to the center of my being. In the immensity of her presence and fathomless stillness, the emotional debris floating inside me was instantly dissolved. Gone was anxiety, striving, and the constant attention to the ways others might see me. Gone was the need to be anyone other than who I am. In fact, all thought, feeling, and sensation momentarily ceased. Without utter-ing a single word, by the grace of her presence, her spontaneous and boundless loving nature, I knew that I, too, am that same essence, that this is who and what we all are.

As our ability to explore and reveal this essence within us grows, we experience a corresponding expansion in our capacity to connect intimately with another. To accomplish this, however, we must open our minds to the possibility that there is more to life than we usually recognize and we must learn to move into unfamiliar dimensions of our experience.

Diving into Subtle Realms

While babies and enlightened teachers reflect our essence and may help us find our vital center, sustaining that connection requires developing channels of perception beyond those we normally use. The realms that make up our human experience exist on a contin-uum, ranging from the gross levels that occupy most of our waking reality to the more subtle and less familiar levels. We might gener-ally describe it in this way:

Gross realms	Subtle realms
Thoughts <-> Feelings <-> Sensations <->	Energy <-> Subtle Light <-> Essence

In daily life we experience what we call "reality" primarily through thought, feeling, and sensation. A constant stream of thoughts are entwined with emotional states—sadness, anger, joy—that are themselves interpretations of information fed to us from our body's perceptions.

Were we to look through the eyes of a physicist or neurologist, however, we would get a different picture of what is happening. For example, when we sit on a couch, our senses tell us that we are seated on something solid. Yet we are really sitting on space punctu-ated by atoms racing around at high speeds. What we understand as solid is not. We cannot directly grasp this fact even though we accept it as true. If our hold on "normal" reality is loosened and our faculties of perception are enhanced—as might occur through medi-tative states, hypnotic trance, or psychedelic substances—we may directly perceive our reality as energy in motion. When the habitual barriers to fuller perception are consciously and deliberately set aside, we find other faculties beginning to function that enable us to perceive increasingly subtle realms of existence. As we learn to dive below the more common levels of perception, we come into unqualified contact with our own precious core.

Although it is difficult to describe these more subtle levels of experience in words, they do unfold in a systematic progression, as the following example illustrates.

Cheryl and David: Applying the Undefended Approach

In one of our ongoing groups for couples, we introduced an exercise in which one partner was to communicate to the other something that he or she found difficult to express. The partner listening was to respond with a habitual reaction. Cheryl and David seemed to be succeeding in this task when suddenly David's voice rang throughout the room: "That's enough. Not another word." (After the exercise we learned that Cheryl chose to talk about her discomfort over David's frivolous spending. She chose this issue because it often sparked an animosity in David that had become problematic in their marriage.) David's outstretched hand fell between them like a guillotine. We could see that Cheryl was visibly shaken. She fell silent, looking down at her feet and flicking her thumb against her other fingers.

At this point we could have turned to either Cheryl or David. This time we chose to work with Cheryl. We asked her what she was *thinking*. She said, "Old familiar ideas are playing in my head: Is something wrong with me? I'm not good enough. I'm not acceptable. Is he finished with me? I'm not lovable. He doesn't care."

Then we asked her if she could drop below thinking. Could she *feel* anything? She said she felt anxious, some humiliation, and maybe anger, but she wasn't really sure. Noticing that her breathing was shallow, we suggested that she allow herself to take deeper breaths. As she did this, we asked her to describe the physical sensations she interpreted as anxiety, humiliation, and possibly anger. She paused and then responded, saying she was aware of her legs trembling and noticed a constriction in her chest that was dull and almost suffocating.

We suggested that she relax her resistance to these sensations, allowing the experience to be just as it is. We further instructed Cheryl to stop thinking—to let the feelings melt into sensations and to let the sensations run their course without mental activity until they completely subsided. After several minutes the inevitable shift occurred. First she observed a very subtle pulsation in her chest and soon after said, "It feels like ribbons of warmth flowing upwards. I can breathe more easily." The recognition of these radiant waves of energy indicated that she had crossed the threshold from the gross realm into more subtle dimensions.

As Cheryl allowed this process to continue without interference, what had formerly felt like a solid mass in her chest dissipated, and she was left with an experience she described as an "inner light." Smiling, she said, "I feel like tiny particles of light, shimmering." She held her hands up, moving her fingers, as a child might to illustrate twinkling light. "It's a little bit diffused like twilight." Cheryl's face was radiant at this point, completely relaxed. What followed she could not describe. She just shook her head and smiled. "It's different. I can't put words to it." But it was clear to us that Cheryl was experiencing the state of peace; the same peace we see at times in our friend's son Dominic, and the same we experience in the presence of an enlightened teacher. She was entirely present in a state that lacked nothing.

The typical response to the kind of pain and confusion Cheryl had been feeling at the outset of the exercise would be to try to escape it, to rationalize or fight it. Because she remained unconditionally aware of her experience, the powerful reactions emerging inside her naturally dissolved into increasingly subtle levels of energy until she touched essence itself, which is entirely without fear, humiliation, or anger.

A number of factors contributed to Cheryl's ability to drop through the various realms so quickly and effortlessly. Being in a facilitated group helped her feel safe, but, assuming the emotional pressures surrounding an issue are not too intense, given sufficient patience and perseverance, anyone following these steps will arrive at a place closer to essence. In subsequent chapters we will suggest precise steps to guide you toward essence when ideal conditions are not present.

Although essence is a subtle level of experience, it is in no way insubstantial. It can be experienced as powerfully as any physical sensation. However, in our daily life, our perception is so focused on the surface that essence is only a whisper. It is as if we are listening to someone singing without a microphone in front of a thousand-piece orchestra. The lone singer of our essence is hopelessly drowned out by the din from the orchestra of thoughts, feelings, and sensations.

Learning to Perceive Our Essence

To hear the soloist—that is, to perceive our essence—we need to become skillful in two areas. First, we must learn to quiet our minds, open our hearts, and relax the tensions in our bodies, basically lessening or muffling the sounds of the orchestra. Second, we need to learn to tune into the soloist. The better we get at this two-pronged process, the more the orchestra becomes the background support for the featured soloist.

Various forms of formal meditation practices teach approaches that help us to accomplish this special attunement, although their spiritual contexts may not define the goal as perceiving essence. No matter what methods are employed, it takes practice to slow down, unwind, and open. We have to work at loosening our attachment to our thoughts, relaxing our resistance to our feelings, and releasing the tension in our bodies.

The descent need not be fast or frightening. When undertaken alone, it is similar to the contemplative state of prayer. To experience this possibility briefly, stop reading for a moment and simply listen as if trying to hear a small, quiet voice deep inside. You will notice that in this moment of focused listening, your thoughts, feelings, and sensations seem to fade into the background. As you turn your attention to what is below your usual levels of perception, you begin to tune into more subtle vibrations. As you learn to abide there, you will come to know your essence itself.

Experiencing the "Teflon" Power of Essence

At the end of the process with Cheryl and David, we asked Cheryl what she was feeling toward David. Tears welling up in her eyes,

Cheryl said she felt openhearted. "I feel compassion for the pain I know he feels when he gets angry like that. I see the little boy in him helplessly trying to muster up a sense of power, and I know in that moment I somehow become his mother, who he felt restricted his freedom."

Connected to her own essence, Cheryl was able to acknowledge the part of David that lay below his recurring outbursts. When we are firmly rooted in our center, even our partner's harshness does not hurt us. If anything, we may feel empathy for the pain that caused our partner to overreact. In Cheryl's words, "When David first yelled at me, I wanted to leave the room. Normally I would have said, 'You don't get to treat me that way. I'm out of here.' But when I felt the calmer, deeper parts of me, I wanted to hold and comfort him." Turning to David, she added: "For the first time I can see it's possible to stay connected with you—even when you are angry—in a way that is not hurtful to me."

In the group discussion that followed, David expressed surprise at his experience of Cheryl's opening to essence. "As hard as I tried to stay pissed off, I couldn't. As Cheryl answered your questions, I felt helpless. I began to follow her lead. I tried to hold onto my anger because ordinarily I'd feel as if I'd lose something if I gave it up, but, by the end, I was wondering what my reaction was about in the first place. Without Cheryl acting as she usually does, with her own anger, my rage seemed to drain out of me. Before, it used to take us hours or even days to reconnect after one of my explosions. This took less than twenty minutes."

The closer we get to our radiant center, the greater the access we have to the source of love, clarity, and compassion. The resulting intimacy and sweetness pervading our consciousness produces a sense of spaciousness and unrestrained generosity toward others, neutralizing the potentially paralyzing effect of our partner's emotional reactions. When even one partner is able to move into essence in the middle of a charged exchange, anger and harshness from the other begin to lose their power. Similar to food not sticking to Teflon, defended reactions tend to effortlessly slide off true essence.

Centered in essence, we can offer our partners complete and total presence, acceptance, and love when they feel the most alienated, alone, and disconnected. What joy it is to be capable of resting in total peace—while fully engaged and participating—as our partners navigate their way through a treacherous emotional passage. To achieve this unshakable equanimity and love, we must learn to recognize who we are *essentially*.

Our Essential Nature and Our Essential Self

In the work of cultivating intimacy it is helpful to draw a distinction between our *essential nature* and our *essential self*. In many of the world's spiritual traditions, the most profound realization, the culmination of all spiritual quests, involves directly experiencing our *essential nature*. Variously referred to as the Absolute, the Ground of All Being, our True Nature, or our Original Face, this is the underlying nature of all existence. It is the impersonal, formless, timeless, and changeless aspect of who we all are.

Our *essential self* is our uniqueness. Think of a cloudless, star-studded evening sky. Now imagine the stars as cut-aways, letting light from beyond pass through them. That all-pervasive light from beyond is our essential nature, and the light that takes on the shape and form of each star is our essential self. We all share the same essential nature, that all-pervasive light, but each of us is a separate and unique manifestation of it.

When we read the teachings of Christ and Buddha, both beings in whom essence is highly visible through their guidance, we see that each expresses unique qualities. While both of these enlightened masters attained a fully opened heart and mind, the quality emphasized in their teachings is slightly different. The Buddha strongly expresses the absolute serenity that comes from a fully open and peaceful mind, a mind that clings to nothing and rejects nothing. The quality most associated with Christ might be called love, arising from a heart broken open for the sake of others.

In the same way, each of us manifests the unique qualities of our essential self. Like snowflakes, we are all of a common substance, yet no two of us are alike. It is our individuality that we tend to fall in love with in each other: the way we hold and bring forth our essential nature through some very unique pattern that distinguishes us from others.

In the words of Martha Graham, one of the early luminaries of modern dance: "There's a vitality, a life force, a quickening that is translated through you into action, and because there is only one of you, in all time, this expression is unique. And if you block it, it will never exist through any other medium and be lost. The world will *not* have it" (de Mille 1991).

If all our ideas about who we are, who we aren't, and who we are supposed to be were boiled away, the nectar remaining would be a sense of personal being, a pure sense of existence, of presence, of "I am." This is our essential self, and its qualities, like those of the baby and the enlightened master, are pure and unrehearsed. Through undefended encounters, we come to know and share with another this essence of who we are. Sometimes the experience is of a personal and individual love, an outflowing from the unique experience of our essential self. At other times the love is more universal, for everyone and everything, emerging from our connection with our essential nature.

Exploring the Qualities of Essence

When we first try to perceive our essential self, we discover that our orchestra is very loud and our soloist nearly inaudible. Because we do not even know what the distilled, pure voice of our essential self sounds like, how can we begin to tune into it? Where do we look? What exactly are we opening to?

Like the wind that we cannot see or contain but can feel, essence can be known by the effects or consequences of its presence, its qualities. To illustrate, imagine playing a guessing game with someone. She is holding something in the palm of her hand, and you are supposed to guess what it is. She gives you clues by stating the properties of the hidden object. After each, you get one guess. The first clue she offers is that the object is extremely hard. You might guess that it is a piece of steel. When she adds that it is colorless, you might change your guess to ice. When she says that it can be very sharp, you may think of a piece of glass. If she were to further describe it as multi-faceted, you might think of a prism. Finally, if she told you it is highly valued, you might put all of the qualities together and arrive at the answer—a diamond.

Each descriptive word on its own does not define the diamond, but the composite description gives us a good sense of what it is. We are led to the unknown across the bridge of the known. Essence expresses itself through qualities that are familiar to us. By bringing to mind the sense of certain qualities, we can approximate what the essential self is like. Yet like Cheryl, who could not put words to it, when we directly know our essential self, even these words will fall short.

Pointing to Essence

The qualities that point to essence are infinite. The following is a partial list compiled during a weekend retreat.

Perfection	Value	Intelligence	Freedom
Wholeness	Truth	Courage	Innocence
Serenity	Contentment	Certainty	Power
Generosity	Equanimity	Conviction	Presence
Love	Discernment	Faith	Peace
Autonomy	Compassion	Joy	Aliveness
Strength	Clarity	Openness	Gratitude
Goodness	Spaciousness	Vitality	Fullness
Loyalty	Tenderness	Pure Will	Wisdom
Devotion	Grace	Beauty	Stillness

Every one of us is capable of expressing all of these essential qualities, but in each of us, certain ones will be more apparent than others, and there is generally at least one that is most prominent. To learn to recognize the qualities unique to our own essential self, it can help to practice identifying them in others.

For example, trying to articulate the main quality that describes the essential self of our friend Elizabeth, what might first come to mind is that Elizabeth is *upbeat*.

She experiences her world in color, taking special *delight* in life, whether excitedly talking about the latest article she has read or a new restaurant she has visited. She talks quickly, as if she cannot wait to get the next juicy detail out. Her eyes flash with her *zest* for life. She is *unrestrained* in her expressions and practically pulsates even when she is still. The quality Elizabeth exhibits is quite contagious—we become *energized* and more *animated* in her presence.

As we try to capture the quality in ever more precise detail, we eventually come to the word *joy* to convey the essential quality we experience in Elizabeth's presence. This is a quality of her essential self. Of course, like everyone, she has more than one quality, but there is at least one that is quickly evident.

As you try to articulate the apparent but elusive quality of someone you know, be sure to continue beyond the first several words that come to mind. Allow the energy and sense of that individual to touch you, move you, affect you until you find the word that clearly articulates the distinguishing characteristic of his or her presence.

The process of articulating these qualities is a little like rolling wine around in your mouth and trying to define its subtleties. Reading a few descriptions on the wine menu of a fine restaurant and then tasting the wines described is a good way to understand this process of using words to point to qualities.

Diving into Intimacy: An Exercise

By stretching ourselves to articulate, with ever increasing precision, the qualities of essence, we expand our capacity to reside there. The focus we place on ourselves or another during this process can be exposing and exhilarating. The dive below what's familiar and known is itself an intimate process. If you would like to delve into this further, ask a friend to try the following exercise with you.

The entire process should take less than ten minutes; use a timer if one is available. To begin, ask your partner to explore aloud those qualities he or she believes are uniquely you. As you listen, remain silent and receptive. As your partner struggles to distill and express these characteristics or qualities, you may begin to feel exposed, raw, or naked. At times this can be delightful while at others it can be agonizing; this kind of focused attention is unusual in our everyday existence. After trying the process with her husband, one client described feeling as though she were a bud rose whose petals were being slowly, gently, and lovingly teased apart. In striking contrast, another client felt "stripped to the bone."

Although words remain inadequate to convey what the essential self is, they can usher us to the threshold of the experience itself. Ultimately the words used to describe the nature of this essence must, themselves, be given up. They must be viewed, as the spiritual teacher Gangaji (1993a) puts it, as "the boosters of a rocket ship. Let the words fall away or they will stop the momentum they've been used to create." Use the momentum of the words to help you arrive at a full experience of the essential self, in yourself and others. The outcome is indescribably intimate.

Experiencing Essence

When we are connected with our essential self, we feel as though we have limitless resources. We sense that if we relax, there is something vast enough to hold us. We are no longer driven to be "better," no longer desperate to meet our own or someone else's expectations. We feel supported and sustained, with sufficient space and resources to handle the tensions and difficulties that come up within us and with our partners.

Because we have all experienced qualities of our essential self, we can reach them again through memory, as the following exercise reveals.

Experiencing Qualities of Your Essential Self: A Guided Self-Inquiry

Earlier in this chapter we listed possible times that you may have experienced a powerful connection with your essence (such as when you first fell in love, a time in nature, etc.). Now, review the list (see p. 26) and choose one of the most memorable life events that occurs to you. It can be helpful to note on paper what you remember. For example, the last moments with a cherished pet, holding her in your arms and saying good-bye, might come to mind. Perhaps you'll recall a time when you had to pull your car to the side of a road because the horses grazing on the hillside against a setting sun commanded your undivided attention. Or, you might choose the moment when you first met your partner, your heart leaping in your chest, every nerve set on fire, legs weakening as though they might collapse beneath you.

As you recall the details of the experience, let the memory evoke the full power of the past, allowing it to fill your awareness. The more

fully you bring the event into your consciousness, the more established will be the essential qualities you experienced at that time.

How was your sense of the world and others different from
usual? How did you experience yourself differently? In expressing to
yourself the qualities evoked by your memory, don't stop at one-
word descriptions. Describe this experience as if you were trying to
get someone else to understand and feel exactly what you felt at that
time.

Take those qualities into yourself again in this present moment.
These are the qualities of your true self, your essential self. They are
always there—you need only learn how to be receptive to them.

Leslie: Applying the Undefended Approach

When Leslie, a client in one of our groups, did this exercise, she
chose to examine the first time she fell in love. "I felt giddy, wanting
to be a part of everything and feeling like I really belonged somewhere for the first time in my life." Then Leslie fell silent. We asked
her to continue. "What else is there?" she asked. We encouraged her
to let the memory overwhelm her, to bring the experience as fully
into the present as she was able. After several minutes silently recalling the memory she continued. "I felt a passion about life," she said.
"I felt alive and vital. Life seemed so good and I felt so good. I loved
everybody and felt loved by everybody. And I felt clear and solid."
Everyone in the room witnessed Leslie take on these qualities of
experience almost visibly, as though she embodied each one. After-
ward, people said they felt moved and more connected with Leslie
as she revealed qualities they could recognize as their own.

When we stop our compulsive activity—in the form of obsessive thinking, worrying, doing, eating, etc.—we increase our ability
to experience qualities of our essential self. The undefended
approach is not really about doing something in particular—or
doing anything different—as much as it is about stopping whatever
we usually do. As we interrupt our usual patterns, our perceptions
become increasingly heightened, and we know ourselves as present,
open, loving, expanded beings. We are compassionate, generous,
awake, alive, tender, whole, full, strong, and courageous, to name
only a few qualities of the essential self.

As we relate in this open, undefended way, we realize that this clear, perfect, pristine, and unwounded core of our being, our essential self, is ever-present. The task for each of us is to listen to and sustain our experience of it. When we bring this quality into a relationship, we reach the final destination of all intimate encounters: "home," the "more" in the yearning for something more. In this domain of essence that lies below our patterns of self-protection and self-presentation, our ways of relating are genuinely intimate. They are spontaneous, unrehearsed, nonreactive, undefended, awake, and alive.

CHAPTER 3

Who Do You Think You Are?

So how do we reclaim this essence, and where along the way did it become so obscured? Early in life we all experience emotional states we cannot tolerate—being left alone, interacting with an anxious or depressed parent, etc.—and, in response, we begin to build shields of protective armor around our essence. These defense structures constitute our personality. Doing their job well, they continue to guard our vulnerability, but they also prevent the intimate contact we now long for. By exposing and dissolving them, we can begin to uncover a more rooted sense of our being and, thus, the ability to relate without emotional defenses.

The Mask of Personality

To get a quick picture of your personality, reflect on how you might describe yourself to another person. Perhaps you would say you have a good sense of humor, that you are likable, sensitive, easygoing, or independent. Or, perhaps you would want to convey that you are rational, intelligent, serious, or someone who gets things done. We describe ourselves as much by what we don't say as by what we do. Our depiction may feel accurate and very "close to the bone" because it is this image that we have come to know as our identity.

However, what we routinely identify as our*selves* is actually our "personality." As the Greek root word *persona*, meaning "mask," reveals, personality is a construct, an idea or self-image that hides the part of us that is vulnerable and capable of unmediated connection. As we shall see in looking at how personality develops, this "mask" plays a crucial role in our lives. It is likely that we could not have survived without it. But we are so much more than this learned self-concept. Knowing ourselves solely as our personality limits us severely.

When we delve into the truth of our personality, we begin to see how our daily struggles in relationship result from our inclination to defend this assumed identity. "If we dare to examine it," Tibetan spiritual master Sogyal Rinpoche (1992) tells us, "we find that this identity depends entirely on an endless collection of things to prop it up." Before we can have direct, unmediated contact with ourselves or with a significant other, we must take the necessary step of unmasking our personality. In this process, we do not give up the personality entirely, but rather learn to wear it more lightly.

Unmasking Ourselves

It takes great courage and dedication to challenge the identity we have created for ourselves for so long. Michael, a southern Baptist minister with a large congregation in Northern California, came to us for a consultation. With his soft-spoken manner and wire-rimmed glasses he looked more like a Harvard graduate student than an evangelical, pulpit-pounding man of the cloth.

As we began telling Michael about the mask of personality, he pressed us to be more specific. He told us that although he felt the presence of God in his ministry, something kept getting in the way of living that truth in other areas of his life. "Could what you are calling 'personality' be what is getting in my way?" he wondered. We asked him if, instead of simply hearing an explanation, he would like to actually explore these concepts for a few minutes. He jumped at the chance.

"Pick three words to describe yourself," we began. After several minutes of reflection, Michael's otherwise serious demeanor broke for a moment and he responded with a broad, inviting smile, "I am generous, sensitive, and helpful."

We could have chosen any one of the three descriptions to illustrate the personality mask, but we suggested starting with his self-identification as "generous." We asked him to tell us more about this trait. "I see what someone needs and I provide it before they have to ask. I am happy to give all that I have to take care of others. Sometimes I do this emotionally, and other times financial assistance is involved."

"How do you feel when your giving is not appreciated or reciprocated?" This next question took Michael a while longer to ponder. "I get mad or pull away," Michael finally told us, "especially if this comes up with my wife, Dorothy."

"Could it be that there are some strings attached to your giving?" we asked. Michael was not a stranger to introspection and, tugging at his collar, told us he was feeling somewhat hot and uncomfortable. We felt encouraged, knowing that sensations such as these often precede major insights. Michael soon acknowledged that some of his giving and positive regard toward others was motivated by a hidden agenda—his need to feel loved.

We assured Michael that there is indeed a part to his generosity and love toward others that rises out of his essential self. The distorted part, emerging from his personality structure, is his *need to be seen as a giving person* and his attachment to the benefits he expects from promoting that self-image. That is, the personality uses giving to others as a way to get love. That's why we call the personality a mask. It masks a hidden agenda to get a need met. Michael masks his own needs, making it look as though he doesn't need anything. When he needs Dorothy to see him as selfless, he is not available for unmediated connection: He is focused on doing whatever is necessary to get her to see him in this way so that he can feel good about himself and safe about his connection with her.

Simply becoming aware of his attachment to this self-identity can begin the process of liberating Michael from its demands and constraints, making him less protective of his self-image and more emotionally honest in his relationships. The next time Michael finds himself pulling away or growing hostile when he does not feel appreciated, he may be able to ask himself what is motivating his acts of generosity. Perhaps he doesn't know how to ask for what he needs. Or, by focusing on Dorothy's response rather than his own feelings, he may be shielding himself from an inner experience of lack or self-judgment that he has difficulty tolerating. By uncovering and exposing what lies below the mask he will bring himself closer to his essence, making his open hand a natural extension of his open heart.

As we will see, the personality—formed so very early in our lives as a defense against emotional pain, anxiety, and discomfort—not only dampens our feelings, it also establishes our patterns of relating to others. By becoming aware of what it is, how it was formed, and how it functions, we can begin peeling back the many layers of protection that limit our sense of ourselves and prevent us from true intimacy with others.

The Origin of Personality

There are many theories about the origin of personality. Some emphasize inherited genetic influences, while others look to karma or spiritual destiny. Some declare that personality begins forming at conception, others say at birth. None of this is as important as the fact that for every one of us, the patterns of our personality influence our capacity to relate in an undefended way.

Each of us began life as complete and perfect beings. In this state of essence, we were at one with our world and made no distinction between our environment and ourselves. According to Margaret Mahler (1975), noted psychologist and authority on the ego's early development, in this "undifferentiated" state, the newborn exists in a state of awareness in which self and other are seen as one.

At some point, however—in the womb, during infancy, or in early childhood—a split takes place. Our undifferentiated sense of union with the environment and our inner sense of wholeness and well-being is shattered or eroded. This might happen before birth if we undergo physical or emotional distress in utero. For example, if our mother suffered chronic anxiety and depression or if she smoked cigarettes, or used alcohol or drugs. The split might happen at birth, if our mother is sedated and emotionally absent, or if we are separated from her for an extended period of time. During infancy the sense of separation might be initiated through physical or emotional neglect or through the loss of a parent. It may occur during the early months and years as a result of experiences as common as straying too far from the safety of a parent's watchful gaze and suddenly feeling lost, or being startled by a loud, unfamiliar noise, or sensing a sudden and intense change in the emotional state of a parent.

Whether the events that initiate the awareness of being separate from the environment are abrupt or accumulate gradually over a number of years, we all inevitably experience this crack in a reality that was once seamless. We feel cut off from others and disconnected from our inner harmony. Although separation from the blissful sense of union with our environment is profoundly painful—leaving us feeling helpless and alone—separation from our internal experience of peace and well-being leaves us feeling utterly empty and disconnected from the fullness of our essence.

To cope with our pain and fear and to fill the vast emptiness now experienced in the center of our being, we seek comforting external stimuli that we hope will replicate former states—pacifiers, baby bottles, stuffed animals, scraps of cloth all might serve this purpose. We mask the pain and confusion of our loss and attempt to mimic our former state of wholeness. As we grow older, we might mask our emotional emptiness by eating, amass wealth to feel valuable, or keep busy to avoid the sense of hollowness in our center. Eventually these ways of offsetting our perceived inadequacies harden into layers of behavior that make up the defensive mask of our personality.

Increasingly distant from our inner experience and resources, we become externally focused, losing sight of our essence and forgetting what it feels like to be openhearted, spontaneous, and joyful. In addition to losing the ability to know ourselves as whole, we feel alienated from others. We forget that our essence remains intact, and that we are never separate from the interconnected, basic fabric of life.

It is important to recognize that early experiences of separation are not wrong or bad. The psychological birth of the individual depends upon the child's experience of separation as it interacts with its environment. In this sense, the creation of a personality is a developmental achievement. But the journey is not meant to stop here. This is only the beginning.

Defended versus Transparent
Personalities

While the separation may be unavoidable, what is not inevitable is the level of internal rigidity or fragility we develop in reaction to it. Generally, more gentle and gradual experiences of disconnection result in greater resiliency in the personality's response to life challenges. That is, we are more available in our interactions with others and are not as reactive when things do not go our way. Similarly, the level of parental support present for us as we undergo the pain of separation influences whether our personality will develop into a rigid, fixed, and *defended* structure or a flexible, *transparent* one.

Most of us end up with at least some personality aspects that are defended. There is a wide spectrum of defended structures: Some are mutable and volatile while others are hard and fixed. In our work with clients, we refer to the defense structures as medieval suits of armor. They do not allow the essence they are covering to be seen or experienced by ourselves or others. In the same way that a suit of armor, while protecting, also restricts and constricts its occupant, defended personalities limit our ability to relate to others directly and intimately. Like a ninety-pound coat of metal, they also require a great deal of energy to support and maintain.

In contrast, it is possible to have a personality that is *transparent*. Functioning more as a permeable membrane, it allows the essential self to shine through and opens to allow others into our hearts. Like a spandex bodysuit, it fits us, reveals our true shape and form, and moves with us without impeding contact with others.

A transparent personality is worn lightly. In *The Ease of Being*, Jean Klein (1984), a French doctor and musicologist who became a teacher in the Hindu Advaita Vedanta tradition, writes, "The real personality is fluid, subtle, and comes up to meet each situation in a new way appropriate to the moment." When our personality is transparent, we remain aware of the wonder of every event, we are not attached to outcome, and we can be spontaneous and available for contact no matter what is happening. As opposed to the defended personality, the transparent one allows our genuine inner strength, substance, expansiveness, and vitality to be available. Because we are not afraid of directly connecting with another heart-to-heart, we have no need to control our interactions, and, thus, we meet our experiences in life and love with a fresh, unrehearsed air.

No matter what personality structures we developed in life, the good news is that it is possible to transform our clumsy suits of armor into sleek spandex bodysuits. We all have both structures of personality. To begin transforming the armored aspects into transparent membranes, we must first understand what we missed during the formation of our personality and learn how to give it to ourselves now.

The Need for Support

The key variable that affected whether our personality developed into a defended or transparent structure was how much support we received during our early experiences of disconnection. As we passed through difficult developmental passages as infants and young children, we relied on the environment, primarily in the form of our parents, to remain aware of our essence. Three kinds of support were critical to the development of a transparent personality: emotional presence, reassurance, and mirroring.

Emotional Presence

Had our parents remained *emotionally present* as we underwent early experiences of emptiness and loneliness, we would have learned that these feelings did not have to pull us out of relationship and thrust us into isolation. Emotional presence is the capacity to be nonjudgmental and motiveless when listening or simply being with another. If our parents had been able to give us the space and time to feel what we were feeling—without trying to change, fix, or control us—our emotional disturbance would eventually have cleared and we would have reconnected with our essence. Our parents' emotional presence would have given us the external support we needed to endure our discomfort until the emotional disturbance lessened.

Unfortunately, most of our parents could not tolerate the emotional discomfort evoked in them by our pain: They were emotionally absent, self-absorbed, or intent on controlling or fixing what we were feeling so they would not be disturbed. As a result, our capacity to stay in relationship while going through difficult emotional experiences was compromised. For example, if we were crying and they did not know how to ease our pain, they may have felt inadequate. We may then have responded to their need to feel capable by denying or controlling what we were experiencing. In this way we learned that to stay in relationship with them we had to disconnect from our internal life. Conversely, to remain in contact with ourselves, we had to cut ourselves off from our parents. In either case, in the absence of emotional presence, we learned that we cannot be fully ourselves while in relationship.

Reassurance

In addition to presence we needed *reassurance* that our discomfort had a beginning, middle, and end. Whereas emotional presence is generally silent, reassurance is communicated verbally, through feelings and with touch. We actively reach out to others to let them know that there is nothing wrong with what is happening. As children we believed that each experience we were having would go on forever. Wise support from our parents, in the form of reassurance, would have taught us that the difficult feelings accompanying the sense of loss and separation are temporary, that they eventually pass. We would have felt held through the experience until it came to a natural close, teaching us that feelings come in waves and will not settle permanently; what we are experiencing will not become the overriding condition of our lives.

Mirroring

The third form of support is what modern psychology refers to as *mirroring*. When a baby smiles, the parents smile back. When the baby frowns, the parents frown. In this way a child's internal experience is acknowledged and affirmed. In the safety of this continued union beyond the womb, the child builds the emotional and psychological structures necessary to sustain him during those times when external and internal experiences are not congruent. When an experience of separation feels too harsh and abrupt, mirroring is like a bridge to support and affirm the value of the child's existence.

At the same time, mirroring certain qualities can also remind us who we are *essentially*. If a child says, "I am angry," and you mirror back that she is angry, at least she knows she is in relationship with you. If you also mirror back, "I see how courageous you are to be so honest with me," you are reminding her of her essential qualities. You are letting her know that the anger she feels is a passing emotion and not proof that she is evil or defective. The child's attention is drawn to her deepest being instead of swept up in passing tides of feelings or compelling circumstances.

The Importance of External Support

Learning to tolerate or overcome frustration is an important part of our development, but children seem to develop best when they experience a high ratio of support to frustration. During moments when external support is available, the child learns that difficult feelings will pass even as he fully relates to them, and that he can remain in contact with his whole and essential self as the root that infuses all experience. When this support is absent, the child is appropriately challenged to contact inner resources to sustain him through the emotional experience.

Few of us experienced the optimum level of this kind of assistance because few of our parents were themselves supported in this way. We became overwhelmed by our feelings of loss and separation. Instead of allowing them to come and go while we remained identified with the core of our being, we developed personalities that tried either to control these experiences or to distract ourselves from feeling them. As adults we might "somaticize," meaning that we create body pain to keep our attention on something other than what we are feeling. We might rationalize our experience, believing that if we can explain it we can control it. Constant activity also keeps us separate from the immediacy of our inner experience. Being overly expressive of some feelings while avoiding others or shutting down to our feelings entirely are all techniques of a defensive personality.

In contrast, a healthy transparent personality with a strong internal support system has the capacity to stay in relationship with the full range of internal experience—both the passing feelings and the abiding essence—while remaining open and available to what is happening within ourselves and with others. When we can be entirely transparent in this way, we experience ourselves as undefended and our connections as intimate.

If we did not receive the necessary external support as children to develop a flexible and resilient personality that is self-supporting—making it possible to remember who we are essentially even in the midst of difficult feelings—we must learn now to give ourselves the support we didn't receive. The first step in this critical process is to become aware of our *cracked identity* and to understand how it affects our experience of ourselves and our ability to relate intimately with others.

The Formation of a Cracked Identity

Adequate mirroring of our essential self is perhaps the most important but often the least available of the three forms of support we need. To illustrate the impact that distorted or partial mirroring had on us, imagine the difference between looking into a mirror that is clear and smooth and looking into one with many cracks. In one you see an accurate reflection of your face; in the other is a disturbingly distorted image.

As you gaze into the damaged mirror, you might at first focus on the cracks and the way they affect the reflection of yourself that you are accustomed to seeing. You might then shift your attention to the distorted image, seeing the grotesque mask that is your reflection. Rather than trying to correct the distortion by recalling the more accurate reflection you have known, you might well get lost in the deformed image you now see before you. You might even begin to believe that it reflects the real you.

When you were a child, your mother (or other primary caretaker) was the mirror you looked into for a reflection and acknowledgment of your basic goodness. Possibly she reflected back to you that you are whole and good and love itself, and assured you that the experience you were having of separation would pass, and that she would stay with you and hold you while you endured the challenging emotions overwhelming you.

It is more likely that instead of this support you saw her sadness, fatigue, anger, or impatience. Seeing this in the eyes of the one we looked to for a reflection of ourselves made many of us conclude that our inner experience was wrong and that some part of us was unacceptable. We believed we were the cause of our mother's discontent. We might have concluded that if only we were better or different, our mother would be happy, joyful, loving, and capable of supporting us.

To get a sense of the impact this had on the development of your personality, remember a time when you might have been aware of some aspect of your mother's unhappiness. It may have been her disappointment in you, lack of satisfaction with her own life, or the inner emptiness, chronic anxiety, or anger she felt. Perhaps she didn't feel successful, special, or appreciated. If you cannot identify some deep pain you felt your mother carried when you were very young, then old family stories, such as tales of economic deprivation or physical exhaustion, might give clues. If you experienced your mother as angry you may have concluded that you were bad. If she appeared overwhelmed you may have believed you were useless.

Many of us carry what we believed to be our mother's pain in our own bodies. We felt too small to change it, fix it, or heal it. We felt helpless, powerless, or inadequate to the task. Even our golden essence could not permanently heal or relieve what we experienced as her pattern of suffering. We then unconsciously concluded that we were "not enough" or that we were in some other way deficient. This misidentification is the basis of our *cracked identity*, one of the layers of our defended personality that we must dissolve in order to be capable of sustaining an undefended, intimate partnership.

Examples of Cracked Identities

The following list includes the most common cracked identities. You may recognize some of them to be your own.

- *I am not enough:*
    I am unacceptable
    My needs are too much
    I am not good enough

I am deficient/inadequate

I am a burden

I am boring

- *I am undeserving, unworthy:*

   I am worthless

   I am unworthy/not deserving of love or respect

   I am unlovable

   I don't deserve to have someone I can count on

   I am useless

- *I don't belong:*

   I don't matter

   I will always be alone

   I will always be abandoned/rejected

   I am not wanted

   I am not welcomed

- *I am imperfect, flawed, broken:*

   I am powerless (defenseless, helpless, weak)

   I am incapable (I can't do it, do enough, or take care of myself)

   I am a failure (I will fail)

   I am stupid

   I am "damaged goods"

- *I am bad, wrong:*

   I am a mistake

   I am not OK

   I am evil

   I am guilty

   I am flawed

   I am needy

We all have a cracked identity around which our defended personality takes shape. Not addressing this unconscious sense of ourselves as flawed or deficient is like walking around with a broken toe without knowing it. Our cracked identity is our broken toe. We assume it is just fine until someone, usually our partner, happens to brush past it or, worse yet, steps on it. Then we explode in pain or outrage. What we don't do is wonder why we are so sensitive in the first place. If our toe wasn't broken our reaction would be less dramatic. We would gently push our partner away or ask them to move off our foot.

Claiming Our Cracked Identities

We spend much of our time trying to deny our cracked identities because they evoke painful, sometimes unbearable, feelings. Who wants to identify as being *not enough* or *unlovable*? However, it is critical that we recognize these wounded identities because as long as they remain unconscious they will control our experience of life, including our relationships.

We have found that many of our clients are resistant to claiming their cracked identities as their own. Statements such as "you make me feel unlovable or rejected" imply that it is the other person who is the culprit and we are the victim. They reason that because the bad feelings and reactions they experience in one relationship do not repeat in every relationship, they must be the other person's fault. If these cracks are in them, they argue, why don't they feel them regardless of who they're with? It is common to hear the following proclamation in couples' therapy: "I've never felt or acted this way before; therefore, it must be *your* fault. This is not who I normally know myself to be." Statements like these are clues that we have just stepped on a cracked identity.

Because these cracks originated in our primary relationships, generally with our mothers and fathers, it seems that the more intimate the relationship, the more likely that our negative self-image will surface there. A one-time intimate encounter will not tend to bring up our negative self-concepts as reliably as will an ongoing relationship with someone to whom we are deeply connected. In the same way, a friend will rarely trigger our sense of inadequacy as reliably as a primary partner. Our primary partnerships bring us much closer to the original experience with mother and father. The depth of connection, then, with its greater likelihood of bringing us into contact with our cracked identities, also gives us the opportunity for transforming these negative self-images.

Matthew: Applying the Undefended Approach

Our friend Matthew has a cracked identity of "not mattering." When his wife, Laura, experiences their relationship differently than he does, he feels as though he "doesn't matter." For instance, if Laura complains that he is not listening to her, he withdraws and accuses her of being divisive. What has been stimulated is his feeling of inadequacy, which triggers a deep well of emotional pain from his past when he felt "steamrolled" by his mother. He does not realize that his oversensitivity is directly related to his cracked identity and not an appropriate response to Laura's feelings or behaviors. If he did not already have this self-image as lacking—his broken toe—he could be emotionally present to her, open and interested in hearing what she has to say without using her dissatisfaction as confirmation that his character is flawed or to conclude that she doesn't care for him.

If Matthew truly wants to be more intimate with his wife, he must heal his broken toe, not protect or deny it. This means that when he feels as though he "doesn't matter," he has to turn his attention to his own sensitivity instead of accusing Laura of being unloving, inconsiderate, and not committed to him. We will illustrate precisely how this is done in chapter 6, "Yearning for Connection with Ourselves," and chapter 10, "Dissolving Our Defenses."

Uncovering Your Cracked Identity

The following guided self-inquiry will assist you in beginning to define your own cracked identity. Although there will generally be one cracked identity that is more prominent than others, you will probably find that you have several. We encourage you to focus on one at a time.

A Guided Self-Inquiry

Think of a repeated complaint you have about your current or a prior partner. For example, perhaps you experience your partner as blaming. Now, consider how you react to feeling blamed or accused. Perhaps you feel scared, hurt, or frustrated. If you inquire into what is hidden below your initial reaction, you will come upon a much more vulnerable feeling, such as uncertainty or self-doubt. You may feel guilty or start looking for what you did wrong. Because this underlying feeling is closer to something you concluded about yourself long ago, as your cracked identity was forming, you generally feel more exposed when you recognize it. It is this feeling that you are trying to keep from resurfacing when your partner blames you for something. The blame brings up your own unresolved doubt about yourself.

Below uncertainty and self-doubt may be the belief that if you are at fault, your partner will leave or you will be humiliated, punished, or shamed, which may be how you were treated as a child. Now you are close to uncovering your cracked identity.

The belief hidden below your reaction is based on your deepest fear about who you are. For instance, you may discover: "When I feel afraid that you will go away, I realize that my deepest fear about myself is that I am *not enough* to keep you or I am *not enough* to handle the loss if you go."

The feeling that you are *not enough* is your cracked identity. Once you have identified it, you have begun the process of freeing yourself from its control.

This process works best by taking each of the following steps in sequence:

1. State your complaint about your partner or ex-partner.

   Example: You are always creating distance between us.

2. State your reaction.

   Example: I feel angry and hurt.

3. State the vulnerable feeling below your reaction.

   Example: I feel sad and alone.

4. State the belief underlying your vulnerable feeling.

   Example: Below the feeling of sadness I realize that I believe that you don't care for me.

5. Recognize your deepest fear.

   Example: When I realize that I believe you don't care for me, I see that my deepest fear is that I am not worth loving.

6. State your cracked identity.

Example: I am unworthy (of love).

Be sure to follow these steps in sequence. You may find that the first time you go through them, you do not end up with a clear understanding of what your negative self-image might be. It is usually a well-hidden identity and is often hard to uncover; the process can be frightening. As you get comfortable doing this, you might want to try inviting your cracked identity to make itself known to your conscious mind. Or the next time you have a relationship conflict, try to resist the impulse to blame, defend, or withdraw and you may find that the nature of your unconscious identity as fragile or broken is brought to consciousness. Instead of doing whatever you normally do to avoid feelings of deficiency, let the emotions surface and continue to inquire into what is below them, always looking for your deepest fear about the situation.

As long as our negative self-image remains unconscious, we think that our pain, suffering, or dissatisfaction in relationship is a result of our partners' behaviors, rather than a result of our cracked identity's sensitivity. For example, let's say we have requested that our partner squeeze the toothpaste tube from the bottom and he or she continues to squeeze it in the middle. If we unconsciously believe that we are "not deserving of respect," we will, on some unconscious level, use this behavior to support our belief that we are "not respected." If we were deserving of respect, our partner would have cared enough to squeeze the toothpaste from the end as we requested. Instead of recognizing that our cracked identity is at work, we tell our partner, "If you really respected me, you'd do what I asked."

When explored, every compatibility issue in our relationships will be exposed as an attempt to use each other's reactions and behaviors to deflect attention away from the pain of feeling flawed or lacking. If our partners do not ask us for help, we feel useless. If our partners do not respond to us sexually, we think we are not wanted. If our partners become angry with us, it confirms that we are fundamentally flawed. All of these issues arise from our own negative self-concepts. We turn the focus on our partner's behavior to avoid feeling the pain of seeing ourselves as defective.

Trying to get our partners to change their behavior is an attempt to create an environment in which our cracked identities will not get stimulated or revealed. Although it may not make logical sense, we would rather feel hurt or self-righteous than face and work with our own unconscious and painful mis-identities. We would rather accuse our partners of "always wanting things their way," or "wanting too much," instead of facing the feeling of inadequacy that gets stimulated in reaction to their wanting more.

We are not suggesting that behavior that is having serious consequences in the relationship should not be addressed. The *content* of what is happening—whose behavior is having what effect—must and should be discussed. However, we will be much more effective at creating lasting resolution and fostering an atmosphere where we are working collaboratively if we first turn our attention to the cracked identities that are being stimulated or protected in the situation.

The Role of Compassion

As we begin to unmask our negative self-images, we can feel a great deal of hurt and the fear of being hurt further. We may also experience self-loathing rising from the shame and assumed ugliness associated with our initial inability to absorb this new information.

Usually, we contract around these feelings. We want to protect ourselves, run away, hide, defend, attack, or go to sleep. Staying with this investigation in a nonreactive way requires something special, something to help us hold our ground and observe the truth exactly as it is, without trying to change it.

But we are extremely vulnerable organisms and our knee-jerk reaction to seeing a truth that is confusing or threatening is to remove ourselves immediately. What can we do about this? Our hearts naturally want to be open, but when exposed to deep pain we behave like wounded animals—our instinct is to close down, escape, and protect ourselves. Emotional pain can be a powerful obstacle to our hearts being open in a completely undefended way.

And yet our fear, pain, and even self-loathing is precisely what we need to approach if we wish to be less defended. "The distance from your pain, your grief, your unattended wounds, is the distance from your partner," remark authors Stephen and Ondrea Levine (1984). Our discomfort is a great indicator, pointing out the places where we are disconnecting from ourselves and from each other.

During the exploration of essence in chapter 2, we included a list of essential qualities. The one called *compassion* is specifically helpful in facing our fears and allowing us to remain committed to the truth. Compassion is the personal ally that will help us take on the difficulties we face as we strive for a completely undistorted view of ourselves. *Its purpose, simply put, is to allow the heart to stay open in the face of fear and pain.* It allows us to tolerate these uncomfortable feelings so we can restrain our impulse to avoid or control them; it allows us to remain open to the present moment.

The human heart is the essence of vulnerability, and it needs a certain kind of inner environment in order to expose itself. That environment cannot look like a concentration camp with barbed wire all around. It must be tender, caring, and kind; gentle enough that we will approach our deepest suffering without defending ourselves. Our hearts need to trust implicitly that if exposed, they will not be criticized, judged, or yelled at. Without this fundamental trust, our hearts cannot really open—to ourselves or to another.

Compassion is the very quality that establishes a safe internal environment. Although this word carries different meanings for people—most of them warm and fuzzy—compassion is unbelievably powerful. It will provide you with enormous amounts of strength in trying times. When our response to hurt (whether the negative emotion is shame, guilt, fear, hatred, sadness, or anger) is kindness, the whole environment in which we are conducting our exploration softens. Compassion, however, is not just another emotion, a positive emotion to counteract the negative emotions. It is an attitude, a willingness to be with something without judging it. And that is true kindness: the willingness to say *yes* to our experience just as it is, to not reject it, and, hence, to not reject ourselves.

Cultivating Compassion

The way we can cultivate more compassion toward ourselves is quite simple, but remembering to do it can be very hard. Let's say that in the course of the self-inquiry above (uncovering your cracked identity) you discovered your negative self-image of *not being enough.* As you began to see the truth of this, you may have begun to experience some shame, fear, or, perhaps, self-hatred. This is the critical moment when you must employ this practice: As the flood of feelings begins to swell, picture yourself as a child, three or four years old. If this is too difficult you can think of any young child around this age. Imagine that this child is being overwhelmed by the same feelings you are now experiencing as you discover your cracked identity as *not being enough*. What would you do? How would you comfort and support this child? You might hold her, sit beside her, hold her hand, or tell her that everything is going to be all right and that she is good and lovable despite these feelings. What you would naturally extend toward this child would undoubtedly be a fountain of tenderness, kindness, and concern. That which you offer so freely, so effortlessly, to this imagined child is the compassion you must hold for yourself during these difficult emotional passages. As you do, the internal softening you will experience will be profound.

Compassion allows us to contact our own heart in a way that lets us know we are inseparable from it. Whenever emotional storms swirl around and kick up debris, we can remain at the calm center. Compassion permeates our inner environment and melts away whatever obstacles are obscuring our essence. It gently, but with great strength, dismantles our defenses and allows us to continue our investigation. So when we are inquiring into something painful, if we can bring in some level of compassion, there will be an immediate softening toward ourselves, an alleviation from the usual criticism and self-attack. The moment the haze of judgment begins to dissipate, we can automatically see more clearly.

The Grand Cover-Up: Our Compensatory Identity

To compensate for what we believe is our imperfect nature, we develop another layer of personality—our *compensatory identity* — to make up for whatever we concluded was our deficiency.

Turning your attention to the illustration below, notice that the defended personality consists of two layers: The compensatory identity is the outer layer—the shield we present to the world. The cracked identity is hidden below it. Our essential self lies beneath these two layers of defense.

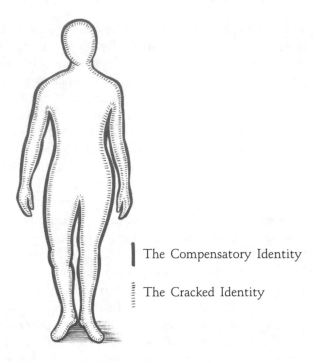

The Compensatory Identity

The Cracked Identity

To illustrate how compensating for our belief that we are lacking created another layer of defense, imagine that your parents were unable to mirror your essential quality of inner strength. Perhaps they did not see it or maybe they felt threatened by it. Maybe you were a little girl, and they believed little girls should be helpful, meek, and demure instead of substantial and powerful. So whenever you tried to take the lead in something—perhaps through sports or building things—your parents may have redirected you toward societally acceptable behaviors for girls, such as being helpful around the house or assisting others in their projects. Whatever lay behind their inability to reflect, acknowledge, and encourage your inner strength, you may have interpreted that to mean that you were ineffective or helpless. This became an aspect of your cracked identity.

Over time, the fear of being exposed and humiliated as weak, coupled with the emotional pain of believing you are powerless, became intolerable. To cope with this pain, you developed an identity as self-reliant to compensate for your supposed weakness. You fabricated what you believed was missing, convincing yourself and hopefully others that you do not need anybody. You spent much of your time and energy reinforcing the position that you are strong in order to avoid feeling powerless. Your compensatory identity has been making up for what you believe you lack.

Julie: Applying the Undefended Approach

Julie, a hard-working, fiercely independent woman in her late thirties, has spent the better part of her life protecting the rights of others. She is tight-lipped with clenched jaws, holds herself stiffly erect, and never has a hair out of place. She is opinionated and judgmental of those who do not share her convictions. Privately she despises her own imperfection and moral weakness.

"I've spent most of my life trying to get myself and everyone else to do the right thing," Julie told the members of one of our weekend workshops. "But I can't live up to the standards I hold. I have self-critical voices punishing me in the background all the time; no matter how hard I try, I always come up short." She feels confused and desperate and hopes to learn to accept herself as she is.

Julie had already done some personal work with us in therapy, exploring the circumstances in her life that had helped form her cracked and compensatory identities. She understood that her father's desire for a son and resulting disappointment at her mother's giving birth to a daughter had contributed to Julie's feeling "not right." She also understood that to compensate for her "inherent flaw" of not being a boy, she had become a super-achiever, excelling in school and subsequently in advocacy work, in her attempts to make up for not being who her father wanted her to be. Julie desperately wanted to believe that being a girl did not mean that she was fundamentally "wrong." Despite her efforts to take on every challenge she could to prove this, her sense of herself as a "mistake" seemed stronger than any experience of intrinsic wholeness. And her dedication to making the world a better place had not softened her rigidity about how things "should" be done. This became increasing problematic in intimate relationships. When partners would suggest that there might be more than one "right way" of doing something or that what was right for her might not be the best solution for someone else, all she heard was criticism.

We suggested to Julie that she stop trying to change her sense of herself as "not right" and investigate what she might need to cultivate in herself to allow that self-image to be just as it is. Julie asked, "Does that mean I'm really wrong and should just give up and learn to live with it?" The look of revulsion on her face let us know that the idea of allowing herself to experience the cracked identity with no buffer produced a sensation not unlike nails on a chalkboard. She didn't want to *feel* it, she wanted to *get rid of it.*

Over the course of the weekend, Julie realized that all of her efforts to change, fix, improve, or control this cracked identity had failed: Despite her striving to be perfect and to live a life beyond reproach, she still felt "bad" and "wrong" at her core. At last, when she felt she had nothing left to lose, she gave up trying to hold her morally superior image together and began to allow it to crumble.

All the people in the room gave Julie their full attention as she sat in her chair, eyes open but focused within, her breath shallow, her face without expression. We could see that her outer defense structure—her striving for perfection—was beginning to give way as she realized that her efforts during the weekend were not producing what she had hoped. As she approached the end of the workshop, her striving was replaced by a growing sense of hopelessness. This began to bring her cracked identity to the surface.

As Julie's once well-hidden feelings of incompetence began to surface, we instructed her to resist the temptation to conclude that experiencing her cracked identity would mean that she was defective. We reassured her that this was a passing experience and that allowing this process to unfold would bring the deeper understanding she longed for. We further encouraged Julie to remember that even at the most fearful and intense points, she was inherently good and whole, thus ensuring that appropriate mirroring was available.

At the same time, exposing herself in the presence of a group committed to helping themselves and each other see through these negative self-concepts, gave Julie the external emotional presence that would help her develop the internal support she needed to face this frightening place inside. Paradoxically, having our vulnerable inner identities witnessed by others, while increasing the intensity of our fear, also provides us with the needed fuel to see below our negative self-concepts to reveal our essential wholeness.

With all three levels of external support in place, the group waited and wondered. As facilitators of this process, we knew that the rest was up to Julie. Would she be able to allow her compensatory identity to fall completely away, even if only for several moments? As is often the case, just as that question drifts into our minds the participant in the proverbial "hot seat" rises to the task.

"I'm tired of putting myself down, punishing myself, telling myself I'm worthless. But I can't stop it." We invited her to simply let it be as it is: "Don't try to interrupt the feelings, invite them in." From the outside, Julie looked like a cup filling up with something dark and scary. Later, several members of the group would comment that they felt a cold chill in their bodies at this point in the process.

"I'm scared and really alone. It's dark. I feel like I'm floating in space with no one there to comfort me. This is a horrible place. I don't want to be here." Holding her head in her hands, Julie began gasping, as though she could not catch her breath. "I feel like I'm suffocating." Then, holding her stomach, she moaned and said she felt desperate. "I want to dig a hole and hide. I don't feel like I can stand it." She began to rock back and forth in her chair. Again we invited her to resist fighting the experience. "Let it move through you," we told her. Shortly after she grew still.

The part of the process that happened next never ceases to amaze those on this journey. When we stop trying to change, fix, shut down, or distract ourselves from experiencing our cracked identities, they too give way and crumble. This can take two minutes or several hours, but a shift will eventually occur, because what is really happening is a reenactment of the event that resulted in our cracked identity as children, when we did not receive the support we needed from our parents. These terribly formidable and onerous feelings may seem real, but they are just old movies that cannot hurt us, and if we stay with them, they will, as Julie discovered, pass.

After the unmediated and undefended level of connection with her fear and sense of alienation, an authentic experience of surrender began to emerge. As Julie faced what was most threatening, a deeper, more expanded and rooted sense of self became apparent. In her words: "I feel lighter now. Like a breeze is passing through me. I even feel a little excited. What I thought would be completely devastating isn't. I feel more balanced and full. I can hardly believe what I'm feeling right now. Even though I know that nothing has changed outside of me, I personally feel more accepting of the imperfections inside. I feel less driven to change others or myself. Things feel OK. *I* feel OK. I can still hear the self-critical voices in my head, but they are not as overpowering."

Julie discovered that below the identity of being "not right" is the unbroken, whole, and complete experience of her essential self. In contact with this inner well of fullness she had the support she needed to endure her feelings of being fundamentally flawed until they passed.

Compensatory Identities versus Essential Qualities

Our compensatory identities actually *imitate* what we already are. We try to make up for our belief that we are wrong by proving that we are right. Or we try to make up for the belief that we are stupid by trying to appear intellectual. We compensate for whatever we believe is missing. We camouflage our cracks with our compensatory behaviors. The truth is, we are not missing anything except the ability to connect with what has always been there—our essential self. In order to re-establish contact with this ever-present, deeper layer of our being, we must learn to recognize and be willing to drop its imitation, the mask that is covering it.

In our work with clients, the question is often asked how one can tell the difference between compensating (or imitating) and expressing an authentic aspect of being. For example, how do we know when we are content (the essential state) or simply identifying with being "easygoing" (the personality's imitation)? It may help to review the following:

The Essential Quality	The Imitation
Autonomy	Independence
Contentment	Easygoing
Devotion	Compliance
Discernment	Judgment
Faith	Trust
Grace	Luck
Gratitude	Appreciation
Joy	Optimism
Peace	Calm

Presence	Attention
Truth	Honesty
Unconditional Love	Attached Love
Value	Self-esteem
Pure Will	Willpower
Wisdom	Mental Knowing

Making the distinction between the simulated version of the essential quality and the real thing—like the difference between false gold and real gold—grows clearer with experience. At the beginning, the best way to distinguish the difference is by recognizing that when we are compensating, we feel a bit insecure, rigid, and defensive. We have little tolerance for being seen any way other than how we see ourselves. There is an inner sense that what we are putting forward lacks substance and can crumble if we are questioned or feel pressured from the outside, especially from an intimate partner. For example, if we are conflict avoidant, we want to be seen as calm. This is our personality mask. The moment there is conflict in our environment we withdraw or explode. Unlike the essential quality that calm attempts to simulate—namely, peace—our "calm" can be disturbed. This compensatory identity is a fragile structure, because it is fabricated on top of a gaping hole. It is like landfill, and we know it is unstable.

On the other hand, when we express the authentic part of ourselves, we feel full, substantial, and open to examination. We don't hesitate to explore what's being questioned or confronted. We know our internal support system is adequate. For example, if we were grounded in our essential quality of openness and our partner criticized or confronted us about being out of control, we would have two concurrent responses. First, we would be more than willing to explore what our partners perceived about our behavior that we might not have recognized. Our openness would be expressed through our curiosity and interest in asking questions of ourselves and our partners in an effort to explore what they were saying. Second, we would remain connected with our ability to create an open, loving environment. If our partner wants to explore what has given rise to the criticism, we would remain fully present and available to the process. We would not feel emotionally reactive or defensive, nor wish to withdraw.

Common Compensatory Identities

Below is a list of some common compensatory identities. In the same way that we generally have more than one cracked identity, we have more than one compensatory self-concept, although one or two are often dominant in our primary partnerships. Which of these seem familiar to you?

The Angry One	Athlete	Bad Boy/Girl
Caretaker	Controller	Diplomat
Drama Queen/King	Easygoing	The Existentialist
Entertainer	Fixer	Good Little Girl/Boy
Healer	Inept/Sickly Type	Independent
Intellectual	Interrogator	The Invisible One
Irresponsible	Know-It-All	Martyr
Overachiever	Peacemaker	People Pleaser
Perfectionist	Rational/Analyst	Rebel/Troublemaker
Rescuer	Righteous One	Seductress/Vixen
Strong Silent Type	Student	Super Competent
Teacher	Victim	Warrior

To pinpoint more exactly which compensatory identities you have adopted, you might reflect on the way you like to be seen by others and by yourself. You may like to see yourself as intelligent, sensitive, or caring. You may like to appear to others as rational, successful, or competent. How do you describe yourself? What image do you present to the world? This will often describe your compensatory identity.

Your compensatory identity can also be revealed by examining the ways you try to get attention and approval from your partner. What do you do? Do you cook dinner for your partner (i.e., Caretaker)? Do you ask questions (Interrogator)? Do you try to be good (Good Little Girl/Boy)? Do you overachieve and overproduce (Overachiever)? Do you isolate and withdraw (Strong Silent Type)? Do you get angry (Rebel/Troublemaker or The Angry One)? When these behaviors and strategies are intentionally or unconsciously employed to stimulate a particular response from our partners, namely a positive experience of ourselves, then we are trying to get support for our compensatory identities.

Although mistaking our compensations for intrinsic character-istics has kept us from expressing our essential self, it has nonethe-less played a vital role. Not only has it helped us cope with early painful experiences, but it has led us to the point where we are capa-ble of seeing who we are beyond our behaviors and reactions.

Stop, Look, and Listen

For simplicity, we have concentrated on the two main layers of the defended personality. As we become more conscious of our compen-satory and cracked identities, however, we will discover that each, in turn, consists of many additional layers of emotional protection. Our personality is a bit like mica, a stone-like material that is made up of many transparent leaves of mineral silicates. Mica appears, at first, to be a solid block, but, on closer examination, we discover that it con-sists of thin leaves that separate readily when handled. Becoming aware of and dismantling the many layers of defense repeatedly brings us to the foundation of our humanity, where we experience all exchanges and interactions with an exquisite depth of feeling and care.

Each and every instance of emotional friction has the power to reinforce your compensatory identity or weaken it. To move toward greater intimacy, whenever you find yourself believing you are right and your partner is wrong, you must do three things: Stop, look, and listen.

Stop Habitual Reactions

Stop or at least slow down whatever reaction you are having. This means if you normally withdraw, stay present. If you normally close your heart, encourage yourself to stay open. If you habitually withhold, disclose. If you tend to attack, take a deep breath and be still.

Look at Yourself

Then, look at yourself, not your partner. Inquire into your reac-tion and investigate whether your perspective is keeping you defended. Here are three reliable questions that will help your exploration:

1. What self-image is threatened in this interaction? (This is your compensatory identity.)

2. What self-image is revealed that evokes shame, humiliation, or embarrassment? (This is your cracked identity or "broken toe.")

3. What inner support do you feel you need to tolerate the experience identified in No. 2 above? (This is the essential quality you feel you have lost.)

Listen Deeply

As you ask yourself the three questions above, *listen* deeply. Try to dive below the barrage of thoughts, feelings, and sensations, tuning into the more subtle frequencies that emerge when approaching the domain of essence. If you cannot experience your essence in the confusion of the moment, simply remember there is a whole and undisturbed ground of being, one that lies below the turbulence you are experiencing. Listen for the part of you that is unaffected by what just happened, the part that is larger than your reaction.

Finally, allow yourself to come back into communication with your partner—less defended and less attached to protection—and see whether your experience of yourself and your partner has changed. Have you been able to pierce the shield of your armor? Sometimes the answer will be yes; other times the power of the reaction will be too strong. If you are unable to interrupt your defenses, do not use this as an opportunity to persecute yourself. Be patient and compassionate.

Jeff and Samantha: Applying the Undefended Approach

Every step and choice in this process has the potential to produce an emotionally intimate result. Jeff, one of our clients, described what happened when he remembered to stop, look, and listen. "I gave Samantha a dollar for the bridge toll and she said—I thought sarcastically—'Can you spare it?' I felt that old familiar rush of adrenaline. Was it anger or shame? I wanted to accuse her of being hurtful and sarcastic but I stopped." In the midst of what was sure to escalate into a knock-down, drag-out fight with his partner, Jeff turned his attention inward.

Jeff asked Samantha to listen to him, and not to interrupt him until he told her he was finished. He began by wondering out loud why, even if Samantha was being sarcastic, he was encountering so much pent-up emotion about what she said. He knew that her comment challenged his compensatory identity as Good Little Boy. Then he realized that he felt unappreciated and taken advantage of. Resisting the impulse to get mad at Samantha or shut down, Jeff began to collapse into his negative self-concept of being "useless." Simply recognizing this to be his cracked identity rather than the most authentic view of himself, he started to feel some relief. Why? Because in the moment of making this connection, Jeff knew that what he was feeling was within his control to resolve; it no longer depended on how Samantha behaved. Her remark pointed out his broken toe, something he was committed to healing.

As he disclosed what he was feeling to Samantha and allowed himself to experience, not change, his discomfort, the inevitable shift occurred. "I was feeling naked, really naked. Stripped bare. I was not feeling hardened against her like I normally feel. It was startling to experience myself so unprotected. I felt younger, more fluid and flexible. Then I had this great insight: My 'broken toe' of 'being useless' takes over every time Samantha is short-tempered or snide, because on some unconscious level I'm always waiting for her to reject me. It never occurred to me that she might just be irritated about almost anything else. Instead, I take it personally."

The willingness to stop, look, and listen softens our outer defenses, opening up opportunities for genuine intimacy. We then feel a new fluidity "like lava flowing to the sea," Jeff told us several sessions later. "I feel myself freely moving, shifting shapes, smooth, flowing, and graceful." The more clearly and frequently we recognize the emotionally defended layers of our personality, the less identified we will be with them and the more available we will be to others. Events and situations that once felt out of our control are transformed into portals to our inner wholeness and intrinsically loving nature. As our attachment to self-protection loosens and gives way altogether, we begin to see things with a sharpness of focus, not simply visually, but in a way that reveals the interconnected nature of everything and everyone. This is the beginning of sustained intimacy. Our future is no longer a repetition of our past, but is unrehearsed, a fresh experience in which each moment is met as it unfolds in the present.

CHAPTER 4

Beginning the Journey to Undefended Loving

As we have seen, our capacity for deeper connection lies in being able to release ourselves from identification with our defended personality. We have already taken some crucial steps toward doing this by learning to distinguish our essential self from the identity we present to the world. But until we can recognize and interrupt the *emotional survival strategies* that keep the whole structure of our defended personality in place, we may find that we are simply reenacting these strategies—actually *adding* layers of defense. For example, every time we seek approval, we reinforce the belief that we are "not good enough." Each time we look to another to tell us we are not to blame, we deepen our belief that we are "at fault." Only when we learn to identify and discontinue these emotional survival strategies will we achieve the continuous experience of the intimacy we desire.

The repetitive behaviors that make up our strategies for emotional survival are so automatic that we are often unaware of how constantly they operate and how successful they are at distancing us from others. In the words of one client, "My survival mechanisms are shaved and showered before I even wake up in the morning." Our attempts to control our internal experience and our partners' responses to us seem so natural that we may initially have difficulty recognizing the extent to which all our interactions are orchestrated by survival concerns. When we try to relate to our partners with our multiple layers of protective padding in place, it is as if we are trying to hug them through ten layers of overcoats. Our outer layers may meet, but our longing to be deeply connected remains unfulfilled.

As we shed our mantles of protection, we slowly shift our "center of gravity" away from personality and toward essence. The more rooted we become in the domain of essence, the more capable we are of being nonreactive, openhearted, and loving in our relationships.

The Focus of Personality-Centered Relationships

Virtually all of us come to our relationships with a distorted image of who we are. Having lost access to our essential self, we mistakenly believe that we are inherently missing something that someone else will be able to provide for us. We search for our "other half," or "better half," to heal and complete us. Rather than identifying with our full and vital essence, which is always available but hidden within the core of our being, we spend our time trying to get today what we didn't get "yesterday," when we were children.

We determine the value of our relationships according to how well they help us compensate for our sense of loss and inadequacy. Let's say that when we were children, we did not experience our parents as emotionally available for us. As adults, we might demand that our partners be effusive or enthusiastic in response to us, attempting to get now what we did not or could not secure then. Or, we may have given up on the possibility of receiving what we want entirely, protecting our hearts to the degree that our significant others can have no emotional effect on us whatsoever.

Alternatively, we might use our adult relationships to reject something we received as children but did not want. If, for example, we experienced our parents as critical and verbally abusive when we were young, as adults we might seek to redress that experience by demanding that our partners make us feel accepted, safe, or worthy of love. A remark even remotely critical can leave us feeling mortally wounded or morally outraged. Our response is disproportionate to the circumstance because we have not fully healed from our childhood legacy of deprivation and disappointment. We still carry with us the sense that we are bad or lacking. Instead of recognizing this as a sign that our cracked identities are surfacing, we oblige our partners to protect us from our own feelings of shame or rage by demanding that no criticism, judgment, or blame pass between us. We require our partners to fulfill the role of the perfect parent because anything less stimulates our unconscious negative identities and the disturbing emotional reactions that are stored within us.

We are fixated on getting the positive feelings that result from attention and approval because these leave our cracked identities hidden safely away. Whenever we feel affirmed and accepted, we feel good about ourselves. When we are ignored or misunderstood, we can fall completely apart. We avoid the negative feelings resulting from disapproval and loss because they bring us face-to-face with our cracked identities. As we pursue positive feelings and avoid bad ones, we are trying to control how others see us and how we feel about ourselves.

Relationship is an ideal context in which to heal the childhood experience of separation that created our cracked identities. Until that healing takes place, we are at the mercy of our mistaken identities, and our partners become victims of our agenda to protect ourselves from further pain.

The Preoccupations That Drive Us

Because we feel separate from our wholeness, we desperately and frantically look for something outside ourselves to fill the overwhelming sense of emptiness inside. Within any given week, we might manufacture an endless array of needs and wants to fill this emptiness or distract us from it. We could want respect, attention, emotional support, approval, or to be taken seriously by someone.

Most of our wants come and go, unfulfilled and forgotten. But some of them haunt us, week after week, year after year. These are our defended personality's *preoccupations*, compulsive needs with a driven or charged quality to them. We simply have to have whatever it is we want, and our sense of desperation increases the more we think we are not going to get it. Preoccupations reflect the personality's need to compensate for what it feels it lacks. But focusing on our preoccupations keeps us functionally blind. We cannot see or connect with our partners' essential qualities when we are so fixated on obtaining a particular response from them.

Joshua and Eve: Applying the Undefended Approach

Like so many aspects of our compensatory identities, these pre-occupations are, for the most part, unconscious. When they remain so, and we build our lives around them, the outcome can be tragic. Joshua and Eve met while attending the University of Chicago, married, and moved to Arizona where they started a successful consulting practice and a family. They felt "very close and connected most of the time." But there was an undetected land mine in their relationship: Joshua's cracked identity as "unlovable" stimulated his preoccupation to feel loved.

Joshua would accuse Eve repeatedly of not loving him. When she protested and argued to convince him of her love, he would be satisfied, but only for the moment. "Every day I'd have to reassure him that I loved him," Eve told us. "In the beginning, that was OK with me." Eve assumed that because Joshua's mother had died when he was a little boy, he was unusually insecure, and she believed that eventually her steadfast love would help him grow beyond his sense of loss.

However, Joshua's repeated challenge that Eve prove her love "started getting old," she admitted. "I felt burdened by his need for constant reassurance. Sometimes he'd come to me with this whipped expression on his face, whining that I didn't love him. Other times he was suspicious of me, as if I was sleeping around or something. Each day he'd tell me how much I didn't love him. When you hear that every day, you start to believe it's true. I began to think that maybe he was right; maybe I didn't love him."

Joshua and Eve separated and, shortly thereafter, divorced. Eleven years later, neither has remarried. Of course, Eve's own cracked identity (hers was the belief that she is powerless, which fueled the drive to see herself as capable of healing Joshua) also contributed to the couple's dynamic. Their story illustrates what can happen when our compensatory identities enter into our relationships. Our partners become both the source of validation and the potential threat to the entire fabricated structure of the person we believe ourselves to be.

As is true of Joshua, if our essential quality of being inherently lovable was not supported in our family of origin or reflected back to us, we might spend our lives searching for proof that we are worthy of love. If our essential quality of innocence was not reflected back or supported, we might become preoccupied with getting others to see us as right or blameless. If we didn't experience ourselves as intelligent, our preoccupation may be to seek out a relationship in which we feel clever, smart, or creative. Our personality's preoccupations shape our thoughts, experiences, and actions in such a way that our life's purpose becomes the fulfillment of these limited and repetitive formulations. When we assess all our interactions in the light of whether they make us feel lovable, innocent, intelligent, we miss out on many opportunities to enjoy what is right there before us.

We are so determined to avoid feeling the kind of emotional exposure we felt as children that we hide our tender hearts from one another, which of course eliminates the possibility for genuine intimacy. We cannot have an unobstructed connection with another person through a complex defense system that was designed to avoid direct experience.

Discovering Our Preoccupations

The ability to identify our preoccupations is critical as we shift from personality-centered to essence-centered relating. The following self-inquiry will help you identify your preoccupations, which is the critical first step in understanding the ways in which our survival strategies limit our ability to love and be fully present.

A Guided Self-Inquiry

On a piece of paper, write down three things you feel you need from your partner. What do you wish he could reliably provide for you or how do you wish she would respond to you? If you are not currently in relationship, what have you found yourself repeatedly asking for, perhaps with partner after partner?

Some of you will be able to reel off a long list of what you need, while others will feel a little overwhelmed by the immensity of the question. Many of us have some uneasiness about naming what we need because of past disappointments or because we were not allowed to voice our needs and wants. If you are experiencing some difficulty in knowing or expressing what you need, you might pause to investigate what may be fueling the resistance.

It may also be useful to reflect on repeated complaints you have about your current or a former partner. As we have seen, behind every complaint lies an unfulfilled need. We are not suggesting that your complaint is invalid; at this point in the process we are simply trying to identify needs, not determine their legitimacy. For example, if your complaint is that your partner acts as if you are not important, your preoccupation may be that you need to know that you matter (to him). If your complaint is that your partner is always rejecting you, you may need to feel welcomed or desired. If your complaint is that your partner leaves you when things get emotional, you may want availability and emotional presence.

As you consider what you want and need, you may feel tempted to state what you *do not* want. One function of the defended personality is to reject. When we focus on what we do not want, we remain entrenched within our defended personality structure. Be sure to state your need in the positive form, as in the list below. Following are the relationship needs most commonly noted in our workshops and retreats.

Common Relationship Needs/Preoccupations

- **Love, support, acceptance and caring:**
  I need to know that you accept me
  I need to be able to trust you and to be trusted
  I need to feel supported by you
  I need to be cared for/taken care of
  I need to feel loved
  I need to be met/have my needs met
  I need to know I can trust and depend on you

- **Centrality:**
  I need to come first, be a central priority in your life
  I need to matter to you

- **Affirmation and validation:**
  I need your approval
  I need to be respected/valued
  I need to be heard
  I need to be seen
  I need to be understood
  I need to be seen as perfect

- **Belonging:**
  I need to know that I fit in
  I need to feel welcomed by you
  I need to be wanted/desired/special

- **Independence:**
  I need to be free to be who I am
  I need you to take care of yourself

- **Other:**
  I need to know that you will reciprocate
  I need a relationship that feels comfortable
  I need to feel safe and secure when I'm with you

If you have listed more than three preoccupations, examine them to see which ones may be aspects of the same need. Then choose the three that are the most compelling. Allow yourself to feel the urgency that may emerge when you anticipate that they will not be fulfilled. Recall how much of your life energy you have expended trying to get each need satisfied and how it has affected your interactions with others.

Although these preoccupations may be difficult to deal with emotionally, identifying and allowing ourselves to consciously feel them can be revolutionary. As we proceed, we will see that understanding our preoccupations will help us acquire the necessary knowledge, insight, and sensitivity required to see ourselves and others with increasing clarity. We begin to see the ways that they have influenced our behaviors and affected our ability to be loving. The more we see that patterns repeat, the less identified we become with them, and the less hold they have over us. This, in turn, brings us closer to nonjudgmental and noncontrolling views of ourselves and our relationships, freeing us to experience ever-deepening levels of intimacy.

Our Strategies for Emotional Survival

Hoping to satisfy our preoccupations, our compensatory identities devise specific strategies in the belief that they will help us survive emotionally and get us what we want. Paradoxically, *these strategies reinforce precisely what we are trying to avoid.* Let's say that our preoccupation is to know ourselves as "right." Our strategy may be to seek out what is wrong with us so that we can fix it. We end up constantly relating to what is wrong, broken, or "not right" in us when what we want most is to feel "right," "OK," or "whole" as we are.

Our strategy might be to choose people and events that are not aligned with our values so we can reform them. If we can fix everything and everyone, maybe we will finally experience ourselves as "right." But in order to experience ourselves as right, we have to be in relationship with what is not right so we can correct it; thus our preoccupation to be "right" remains unsatisfied.

Similarly, if we have a driven need to know ourselves as "special," a need invariably based on the belief that we are *not* special, then our unconscious relationship strategy may be to find someone with whom we can feel special. We engage in whatever behaviors will ensure that we are seen as unique and different from others. We might do this through dress, the ways we communicate, innovative thinking, being particularly insightful or sensitive—whatever is valued in the eyes of the "other." But these behaviors actually end up reinforcing the deeper, hidden fear that we are *not* special; otherwise why would we have to do so much to be special?

Alternatively, we may unconsciously become involved with someone who is unavailable and try to win her love and attention. We think that if we can just stand out enough she will notice us and choose us over others, thereby proving that we are special. With each temporary success we end up feeling special, but choosing someone who is unavailable ultimately ends up reinforcing our identity as "unworthy." Our preoccupations (and the strategies employed in satisfying them) inadvertently reconfirm our false beliefs about ourselves.

Controlled by our preoccupations, we abandon our essential desire to connect and relate in a way that exposes us to our own and each other's depth. But we simply cannot relate freely and intimately with our partners if our focus is on getting something. An old adage says that you cannot leave a prison until you have recognized it as imprisoning. To know the liberation of intimate love, we must recognize that what we think we need and how we think we can get it keeps us trapped in a limited concept of ourselves and restricts our ability to connect deeply. As we continue to examine the prison bars—our preoccupations and strategies—we draw closer to our essence.

Identifying and Moving Beyond Habitual Behavior

Although the emotional strategies people use to satisfy their preoccupations are numerous, there are some common ones. Seeing that other people have and use many of the same preoccupations and strategies can help our efforts in several ways: First, it gives us some distance from what we identify as personal. Second, it shows us our tendency to identify with what we do instead of with the fathomless qualities of our essential self. Third, the more precisely and succinctly we identify behaviors that limit our capacity for intimacy, the easier it is to let them go and to move toward the corresponding essence that lies beneath each behavior.

The different psychological "typing" systems—including Freudian, Hornevian, and Jungian typologies—classify these strategies in various ways. Astrology, numerology, the Kabbalah, and other spiritual traditions also attempt to map the human being's psychological and spiritual makeup and development. Our chart of "Personality Preoccupations and Strategies" on the following pages is modeled loosely on the enneagram, which is a psycho-spiritual system that helps us recognize these maneuvers and plot a course beyond the defensive functioning of personality. We have adapted it to correspond to our experience with clients.

If you can, try to clarify in your own words what you see as your preoccupations and strategies first, so that when you refer to the chart it will be to enhance your own insights rather than to identify yourself according to yet another external source. To help with this, return to the three relationship needs or wants you identified earlier in this chapter. Read them over carefully and consciously, noticing how you feel in your body as you acknowledge each one. Consider how you communicate these needs to your partner. Are you direct or indirect in your maneuverings to get these needs or wants satisfied? What experience of yourself are you trying to get (e.g., to be good, safe, or peaceful) and what are you trying to avoid (e.g., to feel like a scapegoat, overwhelmed, or helpless)? Make a note of the methods you employ regularly to fulfill your preoccupations.

Now, take a look at the chart on page 82. Notice that the first column lists nine common strategies for emotional survival and the results they hope to attain. The next two columns list the preoccupations correlated to each strategy. As you recall, our compensatory identities are preoccupied with getting and preserving a sense of itself while avoiding unbearable feelings of inadequacy and imperfection.

The last column notes the essential qualities corresponding to each personality strategy. It is one of life's great ironies that what we are seeking we already intrinsically are. Knowing our strategies and preoccupations is another avenue leading us toward those essential states.

Honestly Examine Your Preoccupations and Strategies

Reading all nine strategies, you are likely to discover one or two that feel familiar. Look at the corresponding preoccupations. The better you get to know these, the easier it will be to identify them when they show up in the heat of confrontation and reaction with your partner. Also, study the essential qualities related to your strategies and preoccupations. These serve as gentle reminders of your wholeness and the promise of doing this work—they are the qualities that you are trying to recover; they are what is uniquely inherent within you.

Honestly examining your strategies—without shame or blame—will bring you to the love that is the foundation of your existence. Although often unaware of it, what we are doing through our emotional survival strategies is trying to get our partners to give us the love and nurturance we feel separated from within ourselves. Anytime our partners are not engaged in fulfilling our agenda—and we are feeling disconnected from our essence—we feel hurt, undeserving, and bad about ourselves. Instead of remaining aware of our pain and using it to reveal our masks, we deflect our attention onto what we are not getting from our partners and how they are wrong for not supplying it.

Eventually we come to see that these survival strategies are "one-trick ponies." That is, we keep doing the same thing over and over. Even when it doesn't work, we resort to it with little or no flexibility, especially when we are under stress.

Erik and Kim: Applying the Undefended Approach

By the time Erik and Kim came to one of our weekend workshops, they had already done some work with the enneagram and recognized their habitual strategies. But they had been unable to figure out the source of their behaviors or how to get beyond them. They hoped that through exploring their patterns of behavior during the workshop they might find some release from the impasse they had reached in their marriage.

For Kim, survival strategy No. 2 looked all too familiar. She was a caretaker, always trying to fill the needs of others. Erik had typed himself as No. 3, habitually "producing, working hard, achieving, and trying to become what the other wants." No wonder that at first, their relationship "really worked." He was successful in his career and had Kim's admiration. She felt needed and fulfilled by being his caretaker.

In fact, what worked smoothly in these early stages of their relationship was the complimentary nature of their two survival strategies. Their cracked identities were hidden and safe, and they each experienced what their defended personalities needed to remain intact.

Erik, a highly competitive trial attorney, described himself as "cut-throat" and admitted that he saw the world as "dog-eat-dog." He needed to believe that he was successful, not only as an attorney, but also as a husband. If he perceived himself as a failure, he would have to experience his deepest fear that he was inadequate.

Personality Preoccupations and Strategies

Emotional Survival Strategy:	Preoccupation To experience myself as: (Compensatory Identity)	Preoccupation To avoid feeling: (Cracked Identity)	Essential Qualities Sought:
#1			
I do everything perfectly or according to the rules. I am always fixing myself and others and try to make things right.	Right/doing right Following the rules Doing things perfectly	Imperfect/ flawed Not right Not welcome Like a mistake	Perfection Wholeness Serenity
#2			
I caretake, try to fill others' needs, and please others.	Wanted/adored Needed Generous Loving	Not wanted Needy Undeserving Unlovable	Generosity Love Autonomy Strength
#3			
I produce, work hard, achieve, and become what the other wants.	Good Successful Productive Efficient Having integrity	Bad A failure Inadequate Ineffective Deceitful	Goodness Value Truth
#4			
I reject my present reality, focus on what I believe is missing, and live my life in fantasy.	Special/unique Open/available Compassionate Emotionally expressive	Ordinary Unworthy Insufficient Cold/unsympathetic Too much/ a burden	Contentment Equanimity Discernment Compassion Beauty
#5			
I control my time with others, withhold and remain an observer.	Spacious Clear Objective Intelligent	Overwhelmed That I don't know Powerless Out of Control	Clarity Spaciousness Intelligence

Emotional Survival Strategy:	Preoccupation To experience myself as: (Compensatory Identity)	Preoccupation To avoid feeling: (Cracked Identity)	Essential Qualities Sought:
#6 **I scan the environment for danger, stay anxious, and compulsively try to figure things out.**	Safe Trusting Certain	Helpless Defenseless Ambivalent	Courage Certainty Conviction
#7 **I distract myself through the accumulation of people, things, or experiences and keep all of my options open.**	Alive Interested Happy Enthusiastic Having options	Bored Uninteresting Emotional pain Depressed That I don't belong	Joy Open Vitality
#8 **I work or fight to create a fair and just world.**	Blameless Free In control Innocent	Like a scapegoat Controlled by others At fault/ wrong Helpless	Freedom Innocence Power
#9 **I try to put the world in order through mediation, eliminating conflict, or becoming invisible.**	Present Alive Harmony Peaceful	Like I don't matter Dead and unfeeling Conflict Invisible	Presence Peace Aliveness

The more dependent Erik was on her, the more secure Kim felt in getting his praise and affirmation for how "loving" and "generous" she was. In this system, however, if Erik were to become more independent, not needing Kim as much, then she would have to face her deepest fears about being unwanted or undeserving (her cracked identity). Kim's dilemma in that situation would be that she must keep on giving, even if what she had to give was not wanted or needed by her partner.

The birth of their first child brought them face-to-face with their deepest fears and began to break down their system of self-protection. Erik had reluctantly agreed, after many years and various excuses, to have a child "because Kim wanted one so badly." His expressed concerns mainly involved finances and the fear that having a child might require more time and attention than he felt he had to give. When the baby arrived, as Erik put it, "my worst fears became reality."

Kim's attention shifted to the baby, the perfect outlet for her preoccupation to feel needed by taking care of another. In addition, she began—for the first time in their relationship—to understand her own need for Erik to give more emotionally.

Erik experienced the shift in Kim's attention as a loss, and her demands and complaints felt like condemnation. "All I could hear her saying was that I was stingy with my feelings, not loving enough toward our child, and not helpful enough in maintaining the house." Erik's cracked identity of being inadequate began to emerge. "Of course I felt like a failure—who wouldn't?"

Throwing himself into his work, where he could continue to experience himself as confident and competent, Erik increasingly withdrew his time and attention from Kim. She began to feel abandoned, unloved, and unwanted. She tried to hold onto Erik's attention by using her former tactics: praising him, cooking his favorite meals, and keeping the house in perfect order, while inside she was growing more and more resentful. She felt that no matter how hard she tried, Erik became more distant, barely acknowledging her efforts. By the time they signed up for the workshop, they were on the verge of "calling it quits." Neither felt understood or appreciated by the other.

Through the course of exploring their emotional survival strategies, Erik and Kim began to see how their cracked identities affected the ways they viewed each other and the problems in the relationship. Each began to find at least a direction for personal growth and perhaps some hope for their marriage. During the weekend's final session, Kim told the group, "I realize what I have control over and what I don't. I have control over learning to see my 'need to be needed' as a pattern that gets in the way of my loving and being loved. I don't have control over whether Erik will choose to stay with me as we work through these issues."

Erik came to his own realization: "I notice how attached I am to my 'doing mode.' I'm always on the go because I'm trying to make up for the fear that I am 'not enough.' I've got to find a way to address my habit of feeling good about myself for what I produce rather than who I am." Together, they realized that they are more than the habits, reflexes, and patterned responses they were acting out. As they developed a mutual empathy for the complexity of each other's dilemma, they began to see each other outside of the desperate grasping and rejecting habits of their defended personalities. A level of genuine intimacy opened in which they saw that perhaps they could enter a new relationship based on helping each other by not reinforcing these strategies but compassionately seeing through them to their essential wholeness.

Shifting Our Center of Gravity

Recognition is the first step in moving beyond our survival strategies and allowing more intimate contact. As we see how our various behaviors are trying to cover up and protect the hurt places inside us, we can begin to get past the constant cycle of pursuing what we think we need, only to find ourselves inevitably disappointed. We can set our feet firmly on the path to undefended loving by piercing through the veils of our habitual behavior and by choosing to have a direct experience of ourselves and our partners.

As we become increasingly conscious of the ways in which our emotional survival patterns obstruct our ability to love in an undefended way, our center of gravity, the ground in which we are rooted, begins to shift away from personality and toward essence. We see, without any doubt, that when we are guarded and defended, our relationships become embattled, reflecting distrust and fear. When we are open and undefended, our interactions are fresh, loving, and creative in each moment. When the sustaining and rejuvenating qualities of our essential self shines through us, our relationships are inspiring and dynamically alive. This is a natural process, leading us inevitably to our birthright as human beings—our undefended hearts—and the certainty of knowing ourselves as whole and loving.

CHAPTER 5

Yearning for Closeness with Another

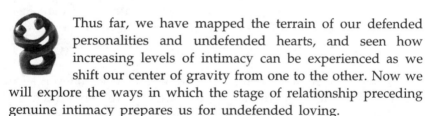Thus far, we have mapped the terrain of our defended personalities and undefended hearts, and seen how increasing levels of intimacy can be experienced as we shift our center of gravity from one to the other. Now we will explore the ways in which the stage of relationship preceding genuine intimacy prepares us for undefended loving.

Most of us measure the health of our relationships by how "close" we feel to our partners, and we measure this "closeness" by how well our partners respond to our needs. That is, when our partners meet our needs, we feel close and connected; when they don't, we may feel separate or disregarded. As we will see, responding to our basic yearning to be close to another provides a context to develop the skills that can forge undefended relationships that reach beyond the usual forces of erosion.

Closeness, as we will soon understand, is not the ultimate goal of relationship—it is a developmental stage. There are, in fact, two levels of closeness that every couple must pass through on the way to intimacy. The first, which we call "unhealthy dependency," is where we are focused on our partners to the exclusion of ourselves. The second is the mature, mutually supportive level of "healthy closeness," the foundation upon which true intimacy is built and maintained. By exploring the ways in which closeness can be healthy or unhealthy, we can more easily make choices that move us toward the fullness of an undefended union.

What Is Healthy Closeness?

A healthy close relationship is characterized by an experience of togetherness in which the couple acts in unison most of the time and has a strong sense of "we" and "us." Both individuals in the couple are consistent about checking in with each other emotionally and are capable of engaging in parallel play, in which each person acts independently but remains in physical proximity to the other. They feel a balance of giving and receiving, and they each strive to contribute to the relationship in ways that feel equal and fair. They are able to negotiate or compromise their way through conflicts, and they make and keep agreements regarding important matters. In a mature and healthy close relationship, both partners feel safe and secure in a basic way. They feel sufficiently in control of orchestrating the depth and intensity of contact according to what each desires and can tolerate.

Couples often describe this partnering experience in terms such as: "We get along." "We do life together well." "We're best friends." "We belong together." These typical expressions describe the common inner experience of being part of a family and feeling included.

In a healthy and mature close relationship, we have the capacity and willingness to accommodate and adjust to each other's needs. When we give to our partners, we don't experience a loss of self, nor do we experience a sense of sacrifice or giving up our self. This is closeness at its highest stage of development.

However, when most of us first come together in relationship, this adult capacity of feeling intact as we yield personal needs for the sake of the relationship is not yet fully developed. Because we enter relationship with unresolved childhood dependency issues, we bring with us our cracked identities and their many tactics. We all have to pass through and address those aspects of dependency that did not get worked through and completed in our childhood: This is one of the functions of close relationships. To develop healthy closeness we must learn to relax our impulse to depend on our coping mechanisms and master the skill of recognizing the ways in which we unconsciously perpetuate unhealthy levels of dependency.

If our goal in relationship is to create a context in which we rely on one another for assistance in restoring our sense of wholeness, then we will develop a closeness that is healthy. Such healthy closeness will ultimately lead us beyond itself toward undefended intimacy. If, on the other hand, our mutual dependence becomes a goal in itself—that is, if we attempt to use our relationship to ensure ongoing gratification of our needs in the form of caretaking, safety, and chronic validation—then the closeness becomes unhealthy. With awareness, we can surpass this shadow side of closeness and move toward greater levels of intimate connection.

Unhealthy Dependency—The Shadow Side of Closeness

When we believe that someone else is responsible for or capable of filling our needs, the natural longing for closeness can become unhealthy. As we have seen, when we are entirely identified with the needs of our defended personalities, we expect our partners to protect us from experiencing the emptiness and deficiency we feel: We rely on our partners' validation and affirmation to bolster our low self-esteem; we need their praise and recognition to make up for our feelings of inadequacy; we require their appreciation of our strength to protect us from our sense of weakness; and we mask our own loss of identity by taking on their interests and opinions. Ironically, we willingly abandon ourselves to get our partners to stay.

The following statements are typical expressions of unhealthy dependency. Notice that these messages share a common platform: The speaker is more focused on the other, while avoiding his or her own inner center of being.

- I try to be who you want me to be.

- I lose myself when I relate to you.

- I feel good about myself when you are happy with me.

- I feel responsible for giving you what you want.

- You make my life worth living.

- You make me feel safe.

- When you are happy, I am happy.

- Pleasing you is all the thanks I need.

- I feel bad when you are angry with me.

- I need regular reassurance that you love me.

Caught in the trap of maintaining unhealthy levels of dependency, we end up living in our partners' shadows, ostensibly supporting and taking care of them, but, all the while, doing so out of an inability to know, express, and sustain a sense of ourselves. Focused on our partners, we refuse to take responsibility for what we create or fail to create in our own lives, and we are fearful of and unwilling to address our unmet needs and unresolved emotional pain. As we avoid responding to life's challenges and dilemmas, we neglect developing our own inner support systems. Instead, we remain locked in an ineffectual stance whereby we look to another for ongoing satisfaction of our needs. We make constant demands on our partners to engage in behaviors that reduce our anxiety, minimize our discomfort, and decrease our tension. Our sense of well-being and safety in relationship is based on the level of appreciation we receive from our partners for all the work we do on their behalf.

When the desired response is not forthcoming, our urgent need escalates for our partners to respond to us in the way we want. We become more helpless and believe ourselves to be victims; we become more manipulative, complaining, and sometimes hostile; we might overindulge in food, sleep, or other activities to numb the pain and distract our attention. Our single-minded focus is to get our partners to comply with our need for self-protection. When our strategies are unsuccessful we feel alienated, experiencing ourselves as we did when we were children—powerless to get what we need, confused about who we are, and unworthy to receive support.

The first step in moving beyond patterns of unhealthy dependency is learning to recognize them. To get an immediate feeling for ways in which your behavior may be overly directed toward your partner, think about how you feel when your partner:

- does not take care of you

- does not reflect you in the ways you like to be seen

- does not, directly or indirectly, give you what you want

- does not respond to you or understand you

- disagrees with you, invalidates, criticizes, or does not accept you

- does not appreciate you

- does not reciprocate

Most of us have emotional reactions to these kinds of common frustrations in relationships. When we are inflexibly *other-focused*— that is, overly attuned to our partners while being less aware of ourselves—we can easily feel mistreated and wounded, finding ourselves plummeting in an instant into a childlike place of hurt, disappointment, anger, and resentment. Such reactions reveal places inside us where our cracked identities keep us dependent in unhealthy ways. Because most of us have not learned how to relate to our inner life, we simply repress the internal cues. When our reactions are emotionally charged, instead of attending to the imbalance and conflict within ourselves, we blame our partners and hold them responsible for supplying what we need to feel good again. Instead of feeling closer to our partners, we can end up increasing the emotional distance between us until someone "gives in" and restores the status quo.

Unhealthy Dependency in Relationship

Being primarily other-focused is yet another form of alienation from our essential self. In relationship it shows up as a need to subdue our partners' emotional reactions, thereby protecting ourselves from experiencing whatever feelings we find challenging. We try to control our environment within a small range of acceptable interactions by eliminating any behaviors that might take us and our partners outside of that zone of comfort.

Although this mind-set appears to be other-directed in that we don't want to do or say anything that upsets our partners, what we are really doing is protecting ourselves from their reactions. This produces an illusion of peace and union. We hide who we really are and attempt to become an extension of someone else's identity. In so doing, we overcompromise and lose ourselves. We sacrifice our self-definition, making self-assertion difficult if not impossible.

Joanne and Sylvia: Applying the Undefended Approach

Joanne, a nurse on the staff of a county hospital in Los Angeles, defines her compensatory identity as "People Pleaser." She pleases others to get approval, while doing everything she can to avoid criticism and rejection. In her relationship, she tries to meet her partner's needs while denying or neglecting her own: She allows her partner to make the decisions in their relationship; she keeps their house very neat because her partner likes it that way; she is a vegetarian because her partner doesn't eat meat; and she listens to her partner endlessly, never challenging her point of view. Below her personality strategy of pleasing others lies her fear that she is "inadequate."

Joanne and her partner Sylvia came to us because they wanted help in dealing with something in their relationship that was creating emotional distance between them. In our initial meeting, they requested our guidance about how they could work together to help Joanne interrupt her pattern of focusing all of her attention on Sylvia. Sylvia made it clear that she understood that Joanne was not the "problem" and was interested in exploring her own part in the conflict as well. Because Joanne was feeling "at the end of her rope," they wanted to give Joanne some relief as quickly as possible. They recounted the following event as an illustration of the pattern:

"We agreed to spend some quality time together last Friday night," Joanne began. "I was looking forward to it." She explained that she had her coat in hand and was walking out the hospital door to go home when a staff physician asked her to finish some patient charting. "I agreed to help and then felt frozen with fear, torn and anxious. I knew agreeing to stay at work (again) would mean I would get home late. I was so scared I put off phoning Sylvia. I thought that if I could get through the paperwork quickly I wouldn't be too late after all. Every tick of the clock rattled my nerves. I was a wreck by the time I got into my car. I was terrified that I had made a mistake in my report by rushing while imagining that Sylvia would be packed and gone by the time I got home."

She tried to identify the pattern in more general terms. "It always starts with me trying to accommodate everyone. Then someone ends up feeling let down or angry with me. I feel guilty and terrified. My throat constricts and I feel very young and powerless. After that I can only hear how bad I am and how the 'other' is unhappy with me. I know my sense of value fluctuates depending on how selfless I am and how pleased Sylvia is with me. When she's mad at me it feels like the end of the world. I want to go away and hide, but it seems as though there is no way out for me. No way to do it right. I get angry at myself and resentful that I can never do enough." Joanne began to weep for several moments.

As the waves of feeling subsided, Sylvia offered some thoughts of her own. "I know I get really mad when Joanne is late. I don't like waiting around, not knowing what's going on. But what I really hate is how Joanne is obsequious. She can't say no. I feel like she is stealing from our relationship to give to others. At the same time, I become verbally abusive and blaming, and I don't like myself when I do that."

Turning to Joanne, Sylvia said, "I'm glad to hear you cry like that. You usually don't let those feelings out." Joanne nodded with a faint smile and told us that her family pattern was to "slap a happy face on everything" at the expense of her own feelings.

Over the course of our work together, we guided Joanne to explore the deeper unresolved issues motivating her pattern of overvaluing Sylvia and undervaluing herself. She traced some of her dependency issues to her relationship with her mother, whom she identified as "dramatic." Whenever Joanne had a challenging emotional experience, her mother would draw the attention to herself. Unable to get support for her own struggles or deal with them in isolation, Joanne learned to back away from any situation that would bring her to the doorstep of emotional distress. She buried her feelings and protected her fragmented self-worth, camouflaging her sense of inner deprivation and anticipating greater rejection and abandonment. Compensating for her lack of self-rootedness, she overattuned to the needs of others and disconnected from her own heart.

We counseled Joanne that changing this pattern would take time. Her understanding would deepen as she observed her thoughts, feelings, and behaviors—in particular, the ways in which her attention migrated away from herself and toward Sylvia. As part of this ongoing process, we encouraged Joanne to increase her ability to experience her feelings each time she successfully interrupts her habit to please others. Gradually, Sylvia learned to stay with the emptiness in her heart and the terror throughout her body as she experienced herself as alone and separate, instead of giving in to her habit of avoiding or distracting herself from these feelings. As she increased her ability to explore all of her feelings and sensations with an attitude of welcoming and curiosity, she learned to rely on her own experience and, in the process, developed a capacity for authentic self-expression.

Seeing through the Illusion of Closeness

As you recall, our compensatory identities need to prove that we are adequate because we really believe ourselves to be lacking. When we lose our jobs, we conclude that we are failures. When we lose our partner's support for our point of view, we conclude that we are unloved instead of examining our own role in the specific issue at hand. Because of our unconscious negative self-images, we are extremely wary of anything in our lives that might expose our perceived deficiencies. We require our partners to promote and defend our self-concepts so that we can feel good about ourselves. Our relationships then become *collusive*. That is, we agree not to point out something to our partners that will reveal the ways that they feel "less than" in exchange for not having our own inadequacies exposed: We don't make a fuss about their drinking if they don't complain about our working late at night; we don't bring up how dependent they are on their friends if they don't pressure us about being on time; we don't talk about the emotional distance we are experiencing if they don't push us to get a job.

If this habit to collude goes undetected, we can limit one another's potential instead of being actively engaged in helping each other to realize it. Left unchecked, the habit to promote, defend, and keep our compensatory identities intact precludes any possibility for us to step outside of the unconscious patterns that keep our core pain hidden from each other. Rather than experiencing each other deeply, we limit our relationship to what we can get from our partners—what they can provide for us—instead of delighting in and relating to their golden essence (or their struggle to relate from there).

The qualities we expect and require in our close relationships are often the same ones a child expects of a mother. This is because our dependency issues are left over from incomplete and inadequate support received in childhood. It is appropriate for a child to be taken care of, to expect and demand external support. Such dependency on another is a precursor to developing the internal strength that will sustain us into adulthood. Sometimes, however, this developmental task lingers long past our childhood, and we find ourselves struggling with our partners as to who should be taking care of whom.

When our desire to satisfy our needs turns into feeling entitled that someone else fill them, we are stuck in a childhood dilemma. A relationship based on the continuous demand that the other person support our self-esteem keeps us from growing up. To the extent that we seek reparation for the past in the present, we perpetuate our role as children, thereby fostering dependency, not growth. Instead of restoring our sense of wholeness, unhealthy closeness increases our neediness and insecurity.

Three Limiting Beliefs of Unhealthy Dependency

When we are operating at unhealthy levels of dependency, the following three belief systems or behaviors are present in emotionally charged interactions with our partners:

- We experience our partners as having the power to make us feel good or bad about ourselves.

- We focus on our partner's needs as a substitute for being directly in touch with our own.

- We are preoccupied with getting our partners to change in some way so that we can feel happy, loved, whole, peaceful, comfortable, welcome, wanted, trusting, content, or any of the emotions that collectively can be characterized as "feeling good about ourselves."

When we are other-fixated in this way—acting out potentially unhealthy levels of dependency—we often feel as if our partners control us. We complain that we can't be ourselves, often feeling resentful or depressed. Until we expose what's beneath this flowing-out of attention, we are time bombs. Divorced from knowing what we want and feeling obligated to meet the perceived expectations of our partner, at some point we blow up. This may take the form of asserting ourselves, which usually means saying no or simply leaving altogether. Most of us know someone or have heard the story about the person who buys a home with a partner only to decide she cannot stay in the relationship five days after moving in. Or the couple who agrees to have a child and a month before the birth decides to separate. Or the marriage that breaks up after the honeymoon because one partner suddenly "discovers" he is no longer in love.

If the couple stays together, their strong dependent ties may give the appearance of love and affection when, in fact, there is little depth of feeling and scarce recognition of the other as an autonomous individual worthy of respect. In place of genuine intimacy with oneself and another, there is a strong emotional need for each other's cooperation to ease our anxiety and to attain a sense of safety and comfort. This results in an illusion of closeness in which the external form of the relationship appears intact, but the core substance is missing. When caught in this trap, we sense how precarious our connection is, but can't figure out why or what to do about it.

Moving toward Healthy Closeness

There is nothing wrong with using our relationships to work through issues of dependency. In fact, relationship may be the best place to work through them. What we are concerned with here is not that we are dependent, but, rather, the level and duration of that dependency.

The ability to move beyond being other-focused requires that we remain attentive to the feelings and reactions stirred within us, rather than turning our attention toward our partners to the exclusion of ourselves. The closeness of our relationship becomes a safe container, a kind of greenhouse in which we feel secure and supported to look at ourselves while we are developing our own self-reliance. Ultimately we must leave the warmth and comfort of these controlled conditions, recognizing that it will be harmful if we try to stay safe for too long. We must remain mindful that these are temporary supports—training wheels—and that our dependence on them must be incrementally released as we develop greater balance and self-reliance. Through vigilant self-examination of our impulse to blame others for the discomfort we are feeling, we can get closer to exposing our negative self-concepts for what they are. We must remain mindful, however, that to develop the inner resources necessary for undefended intimacy we need both support—in the form of closeness—and the absence of support—times when we feel abandoned, betrayed, and unwelcome.

The mutually supportive context of a close relationship provides the constancy that is necessary for us to begin shifting from an outer-directed life to one that is inner-directed. Rather than identifying with our feelings, we learn how to let them swell and subside, like waves in the ocean. As our resistance to uncomfortable feelings begins to melt away, our compensatory identities become less dense and encumbered. We begin to step out of our suits of armor and into a sense of identity that encompasses more of our essential qualities. No longer believing that the discomfort will be never-ending, we can begin to risk being more self-revealing and self-reliant. Our longing for closeness, coupled with struggling to endure emotional distance when it comes, ushers us closer to the intimacy we are seeking.

Agreements: How They Prolong Closeness and Prevent Intimacy

A partnership rooted in the healthy closeness stage values equality; the couple places an emphasis on creating and maintaining a foundation of "shared power" as opposed to "power over." Because we choose to take someone else's desires into account, we negotiate instead of simply taking or being taken from. This ability and desire to compromise, however, can lead to more sophisticated approaches to maintaining our defense structure. Surprisingly enough, one such method is making agreements.

Because making agreements is based on a couple's common interest in resolving a problem or issue, this method surpasses the fighting and despairing experiences that are common at the level of unhealthy dependency. This capacity reflects an increase in the maturity and flexibility of the partners. When an agreement is not kept, they generally go back to the bargaining table and negotiate, compromise, and barter to get the relationship back on track.

This ability to forge and keep agreements is a prerequisite to undefended loving. However, instead of helping us find ways to dismantle the walls between us, making agreements leaves them unchallenged and intact. If we wish to move beyond healthy closeness, we must shift our focus off agreements and onto what we are trying to "get" by making them. For example, when an agreement breaks down, rather than renegotiate a new one, we can instead use the opportunity as a gateway to new levels of personal growth.

To do this, however, we must temporarily risk the level of closeness we have thus far achieved. How this is done will be addressed further in the next chapter. Here we will explore the rewards of one couple's commitment to dig below their surface reality. The resulting short-term instability can be both challenging and rewarding. Because this couple has enjoyed the supportive environment of healthy closeness, they have developed personal resources and confidence in each other that can sustain them during the destabilizing short-term exchange described below.

Jason and Marsha: Applying the Undefended Approach

Jason and Marsha had forged a number of agreements about sharing household chores. One of Jason's tasks was to take their recyclable goods to the recycling center. One week, when Jason failed, once again, to carry out this chore, Marsha, disappointed and very upset, accused him of breaking his agreement and criticized him for lacking integrity.

Jason, feeling that he had been trapped by the agreement, said that if there was not going to be flexibility about agreements he wouldn't make them anymore. "What's the big deal? So the recycling doesn't go out on a certain day. It's not the end of the world, is it?" By the time Jason and Marsha came into our office, both were fed up with each other.

As they looked more deeply into their impasse, they began to see that they had been using this agreement as a way to avoid individual experiences for which each had little tolerance. Marsha couldn't bear feeling disappointed; she had made the agreement hoping it would keep Jason accountable so he wouldn't disappoint her again and would thereby maintain the level of closeness on which they had come to depend. When Jason didn't seem to take the agreement seriously enough, she took on the role of "supercop" and became inflexible about it. At the root of her rigidity lay a deep well of disappointments based on numerous experiences of not being able to count on anyone, dating all the way back to her family of origin.

Marsha's disappointment led her to her cracked identity of being unlovable. If she were truly loved, she concluded, she would not be disappointed. She did everything she could in her life to be accountable, to follow through on her commitments so she could bind others to do the same. Disappointment stimulates feelings about the unfairness of life. Why was it that she came through for others, yet she had no one to count on herself?

Jason, on the other hand, was battling authority issues, which were triggered whenever he was asked to do something. He hoped that by participating in the creation of the agreement, he would feel a sense of control and thus bypass his conflict with authority. But it didn't work. He felt trapped and suffocated. He couldn't tolerate feeling that someone else had power over him. Breaking the agreement was his attempt to avoid feeling controlled by Marsha.

Once they could identify the internal experiences they had tried to avoid by making the agreement, Jason and Marsha began to turn their attention to increasing their capacity to tolerate these difficult emotions. They used the broken agreement as a wake-up call to step beyond their usual posturing and defense and come into full view of each other. Once they reinstated the agreement, they could now see it served a larger purpose than getting the recycling out. It became a barometer of how well they were cultivating a capacity to deal with each of their issues—hers about disappointment and his about control.

Through this undefended self-examination, Marsha realized that she was attempting to control Jason to avoid feeling a familiar and older pain. She couldn't imagine that consciously allowing her pain to emerge could connect her deeply to herself. Allowing herself to come to this place brought Marsha to a vast space of compassion, big enough to hold her pain and grief, melting the hard places in her heart that kept anticipating betrayal and disappointment. Left raw and transparent, she reported feeling a deep and intimate connection with Jason.

In turn, Jason faced his struggle with authority, revealing his fear of being overwhelmed by others. He realized that his strategy to avoid being controlled was to become outwardly passive and inwardly rebellious. This observation sent him reeling, as he realized that the more passive he became, the less he was in control of his life. With his sense of freedom at stake, Jason looked into his fear of being controlled, only to find that what he was really afraid of was being controlling, like his father. To his dismay, Jason recognized that when he would "forget" his agreement he was passively rebelling against his father.

When Closeness Is Not Close Enough

Agreements—and the healthy level of closeness they promote—are often made or entered into in an attempt to create common ground, even though the common ground has not yet been developed to support them. In the example above, the common ground was tilled by working with the distress about the issue, not by agreeing to cover up the issue.

When we have differences and use agreements to navigate around or bypass them, we miss the opportunity to move toward the common ground we share that can only be realized by moving through our layers of defense, not around them. Although agreements may be expeditious and effective at times, when they aren't, we must be ready to engage in the more difficult task of addressing what they are helping us avoid, even if such a process temporarily puts at risk our usual ways of staying close. Otherwise, we are limiting, not enhancing, our potential for undefended intimacy. Paradoxically, when we resolve our internal conflicts, it becomes easier to interact with or without agreements. No longer divided within ourselves, we find that our inner consistency reflects itself in our outer actions.

The beauty of this process is that each stage of relating wants to give way to the next. Closeness is useful as a container in which to develop confidence in our internal resources. But if we try to maintain closeness beyond that use, the relationship will inevitably become overly dependent. At its best, a close relationship can provide a sense of security, stability, comfort, and warmth. But when we are ready for the next stage of development, we must be willing to let go, at least temporarily, of the level of safety and comfort we have attained thus far. Ironically, if we attempt to prolong, sustain, or resuscitate closeness beyond its service as a container for providing the necessary supportive environment to surpass it, the long-term cost that we pay is the very vivacity, energy, and love it once provided.

Some couples have worked long and hard to achieve a level of closeness that many would consider the best that relationship can offer. But even they can begin to experience a sense of flatness, boredom, loss of vitality, of being stuck in their relationships. They report a sense of "orbiting around each other" or "running their lives on parallel tracks." The pain and disillusionment they express is occurring precisely because they have achieved the full potential of personality-centered relationship. They have maximized the benefits of one model of relating and must go beyond this framework to develop something that surpasses what they have experienced thus far.

Healthy closeness is not the final destination of our relationship journey. In its most developed form, closeness will be a result of an intimate partnership, not its goal. Undefended intimacy lies beyond the controlled connection that characterizes closeness. It unfolds when we have developed the ability to express all the parts of our being while in relationship with another who is doing the same.

When most of us first seek closeness in relationship, we have not yet fully developed the capacity to know ourselves as autonomous while also being capable of remaining open and available to another. This level of maturity increases as we shift our center of gravity from personality to essence. Once we begin to develop a sense of our essential wholeness, we no longer experience the same urgency about what we once perceived to be an inner deficiency. As we begin understanding our deepest nature through the nurturing stage of close relationship, we unfold our capacity to merge with our partner with no corresponding loss of self. When we give, our generosity springs from an overflow of our inner fullness. When we receive we can truly be there—entirely present, open, undefended, and available. If intimacy is the flower, the capacity for healthy closeness is the fertile soil in which it takes root and grows.

CHAPTER 6

Yearning for Connection with Ourselves

For undefended intimacy to unfold, we must not only develop the ability to be close to *another* in a healthy way, we must also develop the capacity to relate to *ourselves* in a healthy way. This fulfills the other basic yearning of the human heart—to realize and live from the profound and responsive core of our being. As we learn to identify and then disclose our inner process without censorship, we peel back the layers of emotional defense, allowing expression of the most genuine parts of ourselves. All of the work introduced thus far—cultivating a receptivity to our essential qualities, recognizing our cracked and compensatory identities and their strategies, and exploring closeness as a stage of adult relating—has mapped the capacities we want to develop on the way to living an undefended life. The remaining piece—to reach and express the most authentic parts of ourselves—requires sufficient interest in looking below the surface realities and revealing what we find there. In our work with clients we call this *healthy self-involvement*.

Healthy self-involvement is the capacity to sustain interest in our vulnerabilities and the corresponding strategies that defend them. It is a commitment to discovering all of who we are—including feelings of emotional pain, emptiness, and inadequacy that we might wish to reject—and learning to express what we discover to another. Only then do we encounter the possibility of being seen, known and loved below our protective shields. And only then, when we have developed the ability to be present to the entirety of our inner experience, can we be fully available—and emotionally open—to our partners.

Unlike closeness, which is an outward-looking, relationship-centered process, this is an inward-focused, personal process (although the ultimate fulfillment comes when our self-exploration is undertaken in the presence of a significant other). As the previous chapter described, when we are close in a healthy way, our primary awareness is directed toward our partners and the relationship as a whole. We experience ourselves in relationship to another; we identify with our partners or with the relationship. This is what gives rise to the willingness to accommodate to the other, allowing merging and blending to occur.

In contrast, when we are self-involved in a healthy way, our primary awareness is of ourselves and our own inner process. Rather than self-absorption, the inability to focus on anyone but oneself, healthy self-involvement originates from a deep intimacy with ourselves. To establish a sustainable connection with our innermost, core identity—our essential self—we must cultivate the ability to put our self-image at risk regardless of whether we anticipate a positive or negative response from our partners. Self-focused in a healthy way, we discover who we are below the protective garments of our defended personality system and increasingly learn to abide there.

Marlena: Applying the Undefended Approach

Marlena and I were having dinner with several associates when one woman, whom we hold in high regard, asked Marlena a question that I found startling. Referring to one of Marlena's friends, she asked, "How can you spend so much time and energy relating to someone who is so unconscious? She doesn't know what she feels and makes up an endless stream of stories to justify her actions." Assessing her question as judgmental and attacking, I felt a chill race up my spine. I glanced over to see what Marlena's response would be. I thought she might take offense at the woman's unwarranted accusation. To my surprise Marlena took the question in, reflected on it for several moments, and used it as a platform to discover something about herself.

"At first examination," she responded slowly, "I do not want to give up our friendship. I don't want to discard a friend the way one would an old garment. But I realize that this is only the first layer, one that supports my main identity as loyal and committed in my relationships. As I dig a bit deeper, I see an old, familiar yet uncomfortable personality strategy at work. As long as I keep working on my connection with my friend, I avoid looking too closely at it and I fool myself into thinking we have a viable and workable relationship. I suppose I don't want to see the truth—that the friendship has not deepened in the way I would have liked. By not looking at that, I don't have to deal with the pain that comes up when I consider losing my friend."

Through this kind of self-inquiry, Marlena began to see that her fear of losing the friendship actually kept it from reaching its potential. This was the ultimate gift of her exploration. It guided her to reconnect with the deeper longing to have a truly intimate and conscious relationship with this friend instead of allowing it to limp along through complacency and fear of loss.

Several hours later, I asked Marlena how she managed not to be defensive, since the question could have been interpreted as an accusation that she was unconscious to have such a friend. Marlena responded, "Years ago, I would have regarded that question as critical. I would have felt confusion and self-recrimination. I have learned the lesson many times over that looking at what is being pointed out, no matter how unflattering, is always more rewarding than arguing with it. So today I was able to make the choice to let the question in and see what I could discover by turning inward rather than reacting outward."

Doing this in the presence of others amplified the intensity of Marlena's exploration and helped to bring her to a deeper level of awareness. She valued insight and self-inquiry more than she needed to control the ways she appeared to others or to protect herself from being judged. This is the possibility: To be more committed to discovering something about our true identity than we are to presenting ourselves in a way that doesn't expose us to others, or trying to get others to change so we can feel comfortable and safe.

When couples come to see us, we guide them to examine their partners' complaints in the same way that Marlena did. We challenge them to look for what is true about what their partners are saying instead of arguing and defending themselves against it. Even if only one iota of their partner's complaint is true, we encourage our clients to take that one piece and use it to deepen their understanding of themselves. We suggest that they use what may be criticism or blame as a platform to cultivate healthy self-interest and discover something about themselves beyond what they may already know.

To know our essential self, we must be willing to challenge and explore our behaviors and reactions completely, thereby fulfilling the yearning of the human heart to know ourselves at our deepest, most undefended layers. There is a world of riches awaiting those who can pierce surface realities. But just as the yearning for closeness has the shadow of unhealthy dependency, our longing to know the core of ourselves also has its primitive, undeveloped side—self-indulgence.

Self-Indulgence—The Shadow Side of Healthy Self-Involvement

Self-indulgence sidetracks the authentic root impulse to know ourselves as unique individuals and, instead, promotes our self-image. When we are self-indulgent, we stand behind an idealized external image of ourselves—our "self-presentation"—rather than experience our fullness from the "inside." When overly self-directed, we limit or preclude the possibility of knowing another intimately because our self-focus is to the exclusion and detriment of the other. Rather than engaging the other's presence and responses to help us in self-exploration, we turn the other into our audience. We care about others only with respect to the ways that they reflect us or the stream of attention they provide. This is the typical "one-sided relationship" in which a "me-focus" uses the presence of others for one's own self-gratification and self-aggrandizement.

The following list identifies characteristics that are typical of those exhibiting self-indulgent tendencies. Note that underlying each is a lack of confidence in one's ability to sustain a sense of self in the presence of another. People caught in these tendencies:

- use anger to feel powerful or to create separation

- lose energy and have a short attention span when they are not the focus of attention

- use information provided by others as a platform to talk about themselves

- maintain control by being the decision-makers

- feel entitled

- experience tension when they are not in control

- use distance and withholding to keep their self-image of being "independent" intact

- require that their partners be available for them, while needing to freely come and go as they please

- take their partners' presence for granted

- expect their partners to respond to their spoken and unspoken needs

- experience difficulty making a stable commitment

- are rigid and have little tolerance for confusion and uncertainty in others

- are poor listeners

To some degree, most of us exhibit the tendency to be overly self-focused from time to time. In one of the opening sessions of a new group, we asked the members to spend a couple of weeks observing their own patterns of self-indulgence. We suggested they fax us their review of what they discovered before the next group meeting. Excerpts from some of their responses illustrate the diverse ways in which this trait manifests.

It was William's opinion that he was "the most blatantly self-indulgent member in the group." Notice that even in making this statement he gives himself centrality, a clear expression of self-indulgence. "I talk incessantly about myself and only ask questions as a springboard to speak more about myself. I used to think that this was because I lived off the feedback loop of others. I now realize I don't want their opinions or information about their lives. What I really want is an audience who can applaud me from time to time."

Adelle identified her obsessive self-evaluation as a form of being overly self-directed. She wrote: "I was shocked to realize that underlying my tendency to self-criticize is a grossly inflated self-regard. The more I judge myself, the more I direct my focus and those of others toward me."

Sandy discovered yet another form of self-indulgence: "I rarely feel empathetic toward my partner. I experience her feelings as a burden or an annoyance. This has bothered me from time to time. This week I realized that the reason that I act like I don't care is because I don't want any attention taken away from me."

Even when we appear to be "other-focused," we may find a self-centered motive lurking in the shadows. Shane discovered this and wrote: "I had a lot of trouble identifying my patterns as self-indulgent until I realized that idealizing my partner has a selfish root. I focus on my partner as an indirect means of supporting my own self-image as part of the perfect couple. This is self-focused, albeit indirectly maintained."

The authentic and healthy impulse underlying self-indulgence is to know our own unique character. However, when we were children, our self-interest was sometimes misinterpreted as selfishness or social ineptitude. When our efforts to know ourselves were judged as wrong, our search for what was special about us may have left us feeling "different" in a negative way. Feeling excluded, unseen, and misunderstood, we may have been sent to our rooms, or retreated into fantasy to find ourselves or seek relief from the pain of rejection. Having learned to use separation as a form of defense, we may continue as adults to disappear into the shell of our compensatory identities as protection from uncomfortable contact with others. That is, our original healthy self-interest has turned into self-defense.

Even if we receive a steady stream of affirmation and validation from our partners, until we explore this pattern we can remain permanently isolated on a very deep level. We can end up creating an inflated self-regard that is dependent on the reflection of others. In this place we are far afield from fulfilling our longing to know ourselves, and miles away from the possibility for undefended intimacy with another.

The Self-Sufficiency Façade

Although people who exhibit self-indulgent tendencies appear to be self-sufficient, in reality, they are just as dependent as those who overtly express dependency. They are still relying on the environment, in the form of their primary partners, family members, and friends, to keep their positive self-image intact. When the need for others to provide constant positive attention is very high, even the smallest arguments can produce extreme internal emotional suffering, which is expressed through hostile assault or total withdrawal.

Despite an air of independence, those caught in the primitive levels of this pattern have a great deal of trouble being alone. In relationships, they cannot recognize their partners as having separate needs and concerns; rather, they see their partners as extensions of themselves. Sasha, a client, described it this way: "When my partner feels bad, I realize I'm angry because he's not available for me. I become annoyed that he doesn't have more friends. He is always leaning on me. I want him to grow up so he can be there for me."

One of the most frequent phrases we use with couples in their first therapy session together is, "This isn't about you." In these initial stages people don't have the tools to avoid entanglement when their partner is talking about a charged issue. The "this isn't about you" instruction provides temporary sanctuary for the partner, enabling the listener to hold back a reaction, thus giving the speaker room to explore without fear of attack.

The first time this therapeutic phrase, "This isn't about you," collides with the tendency to be self-indulgent, there is a clear tilt in the client's face indicating "this doesn't compute." Those who are stuck in or are grappling to move beyond being overly self-focused believe that everything is about them.

The need to be reflected in ways that help us feel valuable is a function, of course, of our compensatory identities. We do not want our self-image to be challenged and exposed. Like the reflection of our face on the surface of a pond, our self-image can only remain intact when left undisturbed. We mistakenly believe that any experience of feeling that we are "bad" or "not enough" is the result of our partners' behaviors, actions, and reactions, rather than a reflection of our own internal conflicts and incompletions.

Just as relationship provides a context for resolving childhood issues of unhealthy dependency, it is also a container in which our tendencies toward self-absorption can find resolution. We begin by remaining vigilant of our unconscious attempts to elicit admiration and agreement, and then investigate why we don't invite honest reflections of the ways we have become stuck or are recycling old patterns.

As with dependency issues, it is not the self-centeredness itself that should be of concern to us, but its duration and level. If we continue to look for a response from our partners that will make us feel more positive about ourselves instead of letting their responses expose our cracked identities, we remain caught in a pattern of identifying with our ways of compensating, and we miss the opportunity to discover our intrinsic wholeness. If, however, we can learn to trust that the reward for interrupting the strategies of our compensatory identities is knowing our unique and precious essential self, we discover that the discomfort will pass, leaving us feeling stirred and moved. The more capable we are of probing and disclosing what lies below our emotional defenses, the more intimate we feel, and the more we will want to share the entirety of our experience with another.

Developing Healthy
Self-Involvement

If we experienced attention in our family of origin as negative, critical, or invasive, we may initially find ourselves shut down to the journey toward healthy self-involvement. Our defended personalities may have been organized to create impenetrable shields that even we cannot see through. As a result, in these early stages it is not unusual for clients to feel pressured by probing questions, sometimes venting their frustration by saying, "I don't know what you are looking for, but there is no more in here."

There is a lot more in there. This "more" is comprised of the many layers of personality that obstruct undefended intimacy with ourselves and each other, and of the treasure at the center of these layers, our essential self. As the Sufi saying goes, "If you want trinkets they are on the shore. But if you want real treasure, you'll have to dive into the ocean." The real prize is always in the depths. Our challenge is to learn to attune ourselves to what's below the more conscious, readily available information and to have the courage to keep looking when we think there's nothing else there. Our yearning to know the many layers of our existence—to be interested in the full spectrum of our experience—produces an intimate result only when we pass beyond what we believe into unknown territory.

The Vertical Drop

To assist clients to discover the deeper meaning and significance of their lives leading to intimacy, we introduce them to the practice of the *vertical drop*. The goal of the vertical drop is to ask and answer questions—engaging in self-inquiry—until we discover something we didn't know before we started. When properly done, the process ends with a feeling of open relaxation and wonderment.

Sonia: Applying the Undefended Approach

When Sonia first came to work with us, she was unaware of her essential self, but she hoped there was more to her than what she experienced in the course of working two part-time jobs and trying to complete a master's degree. In our first session together, she wanted to discuss the trouble she was having communicating with her mother. According to Sonia, her mother never seemed to want to talk to her, passing the phone over to her father whenever Sonia called. When we asked her what she felt when her mother handed the phone over to her father, her response was, "I feel OK, I guess." "Then why are you wanting to talk about it?" we asked. "I don't know. I just want it to be different." "Why?" we asked again. "I just do," she responded.

We introduced Sonia to the vertical drop, suggesting she use our questions to drop below the content of the issue—what she already knew about the situation—in an effort to discover something new. We asked her to think of herself as standing on a platform that has a ladder extending down from it to a different, unknown place below. To assist her in deepening her inquiry, we told her that we would ask her a series of questions, and each of her answers would help her descend to another rung down the ladder.

Sonia began by restating the content of the issue succinctly. "I don't like it when my mother won't talk to me on the phone." From there we suggested she try to go deeper, offering her another question as a guide: "What do you feel when your mother won't talk to you?" With eyes averted, Sonia shrugged her shoulders, nonchalantly responding, "I guess I think she doesn't want to talk to me." Sonia stopped and looked at us as if waiting for us to comment or ask another question. We simply replied: "That's one step down the ladder."

"Well, I feel bad when I think that my own mother doesn't want to talk to me. Wouldn't anybody?" We affirmed to Sonia that she had now taken two very valuable steps down in the process of delving into herself. We suggested that she let go of her question to us—which asked for confirmation that her feeling was normal—and keep diving.

After several seconds she responded with, "I'm blank." "Great," we both said. "Blank is a very important place in the descent. It means that you are moving below the outer layers of your defended personality." We explained that when we reach a point at which we go blank, we must resist the temptation to interpret this to mean there is no more. "Don't let your fear that there is 'no more' outweigh the possibility that there is more to discover," we told Sonia. "Find the willingness to venture into unknown terrain. By doing this you will carve a path through the outer layers of your defended personality. You must go deeper." We encouraged Sonia to stay with the inquiry and repeated her first two steps down to help her track the process.

Sitting with the blankness, Sonia said, "This is hard." Taking her comment literally, we recognized the tendency to harden when our personality is reaching the limits of its ability to cope. Instead of surrendering to the process, we tighten our structure for fear we will fall apart. Our intuition is actually right: Something in us is falling apart, or rather falling away, dissolving into a deeper understanding of ourselves. First we harden, and we often refer to ourselves as being "stuck" or "tense." But when we grow tired and weary of the tension, and finally let ourselves go, we open to the present moment, to a wider experience of what is truly happening.

We told Sonia that her defenses were what she was experiencing as "hard," and that this was a good sign. "It means that you are pressing against the armor of your defended personality and feeling its resistance. Keep inquiring," we instructed her. "Use the memory of your mother passing the phone over to your father again to see what gets stimulated about this issue."

"I guess I'm afraid my mother doesn't really love me." Sonia's eyes were moist now and her voice softer. "If my mother doesn't love me, does that mean that there is something wrong with me?" Four steps into the process Sonia was touching her cracked identity and could feel the tenderness and rawness.

We waited for her to continue. Rather abruptly, a cloud passed over Sonia's face and we could see her harden again. Now she said that her mother was incapable of loving anyone or anything. We gently interrupted her, asking her to question the purpose of this last comment. She saw it as an escape and that her anger was an attempt to move away from the pain she was beginning to experience. We invited her to return to the rung of the ladder that she had occupied before she tried to slip away.

"I feel a pain in my heart, sadness, and darkness." By now Sonia was in completely new territory. We assured her that she was at least six rungs down the ladder and fast approaching her destination. She didn't seem to care. She was authentically inquisitive. "I think that if my mother doesn't love me, no one will ever love me. I believe that I have to get her to love me before I can have a rewarding relationship in my life." This was clearly a new insight for Sonia who looked as if she had just given birth, exalted and fatigued at the same time. We all breathed a sigh of relief.

There is no magic formula for predicting how many steps down the ladder it will take to get to a fresh insight. When guiding someone, we sometimes use seven steps, at other times we might use fifteen. The purpose in tracking the number of steps is to ensure that the process continues beyond the armor of personality. The countdown provides encouragement to keep going when we think we have reached a dead end. When the authentic impulse to know more about ourselves is firmly in place, we no longer need the external support of this method.

It takes time and patience to gain entry into deeper aspects of ourselves through the defenses we have erected over the years. We must create a new reflex to wonder about—not answer—questions concerning why we are having whatever experience or reaction we are having. You will know when you have discovered something new. The feeling is unmistakably intimate.

Five Common Mistakes That Block Insights

There are five common mistakes to avoid with the vertical drop. You will want to review this list before trying the guided self-inquiry that will follow.

The "Because" Pitfall

Beware of the use of the word "because." Generally, when we use this word to explain a feeling or action, we are stuck in personality. We are answering the question with a story that will reinforce the narrow point of view of our defense structure instead of helping us see what is below it. For example, "I am mad because my partner doesn't support me when I try to set limits with our three-year-old son" tells us very little about the speaker—the bulk of attention is placed on how the other person affects the speaker.

Instead of "because," and all the personality-centered stories geared to reinforce your position, try saying "I'm mad . . . ," to see what happens if you simply allow that experience to be as it is without interpretation or rationalization. Usually something deeper will become apparent. For example, "As I say that, I feel some sadness," or "I am uncomfortable feeling so much anger in my body." Allow the deeper layers to unfold from there.

The "Explaining" Pitfall

Notice when you are explaining versus directly experiencing and articulating what you are feeling in the moment. By explaining, you are placing distance between you and what you are expressing—you could even be talking about someone else. Bring your attention into the present moment, not how you feel "generally." Try saying, "Right now I notice . . ." When you articulate your feelings, report what you notice as you are experiencing it. This is much more exposing and risky and will bring you into a deeper relationship with yourself.

The Pitfall of "Answering Quickly"

When most of us are asked the question, "How do you feel?" our reflexive response is "fine." In the vertical drop process, no question is answered quickly, because whatever you answer rapidly is generally an automatic response (and therefore comes out of personality) or something already known to you. Consider each question as if for the first time. Let yourself wonder about it, let it take you someplace you have never been before. If clients find it difficult at first to hold back a quick response, we'll ask them to say "hmmmm" to remind them to freshly consider the question before answering it.

The "Listing" Pitfall

The listing pitfall is very common. When asked a question, we list everything we can think of as an answer. If someone asks you, "What are you experiencing?" and you respond: "I feel hot, annoyed, pissed off, mad that things aren't easier, a little scared, frustrated . . ." you are skating the surface, not diving vertically. If you have this tendency, restrict yourself to stating your experiences one at a time, exploring it fully before investigating others you have listed. See where it leads you. This will focus your inquiry downward.

The "Concept" Pitfall

Using concepts to convey our experience keeps us locked in personality. We might say we feel "abandoned," "isolated," or "uncomfortable," but these are vague, meaningless terms in the context of the vertical drop. Concepts such as these can also produce a feeling of safety because we have put a box around what each of these means instead of opening up to the full power of being touched and affected. If during your introspection you feel safe, rational, and level-headed, you will know you are making your experience a concept. You are not dropping vertically.

You can move beyond the concept pitfall by trying to convey your experience in ways that a child can understand. Or, you can cut through the concept by identifying the feelings beneath it, and the bodily sensations that may be connected to that feeling. Articulating your experience with detail and precision will bring you more directly into the present moment, and the resulting intimacy will be undeniable.

For instance, instead of saying that you feel "abandoned," a concept that may have a lot of past associations for you, attempt to take a noncontrolling position and let your experience be exactly as it is. When our client Harvey tried this, he was drawn more deeply into his experience: "I feel all alone. My body is cold, chilled to the bone, and as I look out into the room it seems darker than it did a few moments ago. I'm having trouble breathing and I keep wanting to look for a familiar face, voice, or landmark." Harvey let go of the concept and felt what was true for him in that moment. This, in turn, allowed the experience to shift to ever deeper levels.

While engaged in self-inquiry, open curiosity will sustain you more than struggling to "do it right." When you feel stuck, or notice that you are moving horizontally rather than vertically, review these five common pitfalls. They will help point you in the right direction. Keep in mind that your goal is to pierce the veils and layers of the defended personality so that you may have a genuine, direct experience of your essential self. To accomplish this you must, as H. W. L. Poonja instructed his students, "Go deeper, go deeper. Don't land anywhere."

Self-Inquiry: Taking the Vertical Drop

To practice this process, choose a complaint about your partner, if you are currently in relationship, or select a complaint from a prior relationship that still has a "charge" for you today. Stating the complaint silently to yourself should produce a feeling of tension, anxiety, discomfort, emotional pain, or confusion. In the beginning it is best to try this practice with a lesser charged issue than one that "makes you insane." You are trying to develop a muscle for self-inquiry that will deepen the taproot into the bedrock of your being. As you continue this practice with incrementally more unbearable issues, you will feel increasingly more rooted in the vast resources of your essence. Ultimately nothing your partner can do will disturb your sense of inner peace and balance.

Phrase Your Complaint Succinctly

Phrase the complaint so that it is short, direct, and simple. In this exercise, make the complaint about the other person, not about yourself. To evoke the feelings that will provide the key to going deeper, intensify or exaggerate your statement beyond what you might presently feel. For example, if your partner has a pattern of falling asleep when the possibility for more vulnerable contact is present, you might phrase your complaint: "You always go unconscious."

Here are some other examples of common complaints:

You are:

- out of control
- critical
- stingy
- abusive
- withdrawn
- a liar

You are too:

- angry
- needy
- irresponsible
- emotionally intense

You are not:

- here for me
- available
- caring
- expressive
- smart enough

You don't:

- give to me
- know what you feel
- hear me/understand me
- share your feelings

Establish a Clear Intention

Having identified a complaint, establish an intention with regard to the vertical drop that you are about to take:

- Are you willing to inquire into this complaint and use it to understand yourself more deeply?

- Are you willing to feel disturbing or uncomfortable feelings should they emerge?

- Are you willing to put aside your beliefs about what is happening between you and your partner—to relax your position—in order to discover something about yourself?

Healthy self-involvement begins when you are willing to allow whatever experience you are having to be just as it is. It continues when you focus on yourself first, regardless of how important you feel the complaint is about your partner, regardless of how many people agree that the complaint is justified, and regardless of the intensity of your feelings about it.

Questions to Assist Your Inward Dive

We have formulated a list of questions to guide you in your descent. Ultimately, these and other questions will come to you naturally as you delve below personality-centered concerns and move toward genuine self-expression. Over time and with practice, the questions will fall away entirely, and the process will unfold without them.

As you follow the questions in the order listed, allow yourself to stay with each question for a while, exploring its depths. You might find that you have to sit with a question for five or ten minutes, jotting notes as you go; or you might simply ask yourself the question over and over as if using it to peer beyond some inner veil. To assist you in this self-exploration, we have included the answers that carried one workshop participant named Ira down several rungs of the ladder. If a particular question does not apply to your situation, skip it. If another enters your consciousness, follow it. The single most important guide in this process is your keen desire to learn something new about yourself. The more you discover, the deeper will be your experience of undefended intimacy.

1. State the complaint succinctly, as clearly as you can, in a short sentence as described in the list above.
   Ira: "You are too needy and dependent."

2. How do you feel when your partner is this way?
   Ira: "I feel pressured to give you what you need. I feel emptied out, as if I don't have enough for both of us."

3. What sensations does this situation evoke in your body?
   Ira: "First I notice that I feel tight, as though someone is going to take something from me. Beneath that, I feel drained, like I will collapse. As I say this I feel very tired and want to go to sleep."

4. How is this familiar? What does this remind you of (particularly from childhood)?
   Ira: "This reminds me of how I used to feel with my mother. She seemed weak to me. Although she was not outwardly needy, I felt as though it was up to me to make her happy."

5. What familiar response(s) does this activate in you?
   Ira: "I feel overwhelmed. I feel mad, and then I want to shut down."

6. What familiar belief(s) does this reinforce in you?
   Ira: "I have no one I can count on. I have to do everything for myself. The 'other' will suck me dry. I am a disappointment."

7. What are your deepest fears about the present-day situation?
   Ira: "I'm afraid I'll be trapped into becoming your father. I'm also scared that if you don't need me, you will leave me."

8. What aren't you saying to your partner about what you want and how you feel?
   Ira: "I want you to be different. I want to be the one that is taken care of. As I say this, I feel some shame. It's hard to expose it and let you see me feeling like this."

9. What is the "payoff"? How does this situation serve you? How does it help you maintain your usual defended position?
   Ira: "I get to be right. I get to be better than you, to maintain control and maintain my idea of myself as competent. Focusing on you helps me avoid feeling my own needs. I guess I get to avoid facing my fear that you'll stay with me only as long as I take care of you—and the deeper fear that you don't love me for who I am, but for what I do for you."

10. If you could have your partner act the way you want, what would happen? How would your partner then appear to you?

Ira: "You would be stronger. You would have enough resources for both of us. I could depend on you. You would take care of me once in a while."

11. What feelings and sensations are you aware of when you imagine your partner to be the way you want?

Ira: "I feel relaxed and can breathe more easily. I feel looser and freer. I also feel a stab of fear about how threatened I'd be if you were stronger. I'm beginning to see how difficult it would be for me to have you take care of me. I also wonder why you'd stay with me if you were stronger."

12. If your partner doesn't change, how would you like to be when you are triggered about this complaint?

Ira: "I'd like to feel as though I have enough inner resources to stay in relationship with you while we try to figure this out. I'd like to be able to believe that it's not my fault or that I have to fix it. I'd like to not need you to be different."

13. What do you need to cultivate in yourself to be the way you responded to the question above?

Ira: "I'd have to know myself and believe in myself. I'd have to find a place in me that can hear what you are saying without pulling away or having to fix it. I have to believe that you will stay with me because of who I am, not for what I can give."

14. How might you have contributed to this situation?

Ira: "I may have helped to create this situation to become aware of my own needs and to learn to provide for myself in a loving, compassionate way. I'm beginning to see that the times I see you as too dependent are when I want to be taken care of more. I also see that I encourage you to need me out of my fear that if you don't, you'll leave me."

15. What could you do the next time you experience this or a similar reaction to your partner?

Ira: "The next time I experience you as needy I can stop making you wrong. I can focus instead on the part of me that feels drained. I can use my annoyance with you to measure how full or empty I'm feeling. This can help me look at my own needs. I can also try to love us both even when we are not feeling connected."

When Ira began this exercise he believed there was something wrong with his partner and that she had to change for their relationship to continue. By the completion of the process he told us that he felt substantially different. We asked him to return his attention to his opening complaint, face his partner, and explore his feelings toward her now. "I feel grateful that we are doing this work together. I think it will be helpful to remember that when I feel overwhelmed by you, my fear of not being enough is colliding with your fear of being unlovable [which Ira's partner disclosed to him during an earlier exercise]. I feel some dread, but also some excitement that maybe we can get through this together." Ira discovered that the path to greater intimacy lay not in changing his partner, but in plunging deeply into himself, allowing himself to be witnessed in the dive, and returning to the content of the issue newly centered in essence.

If after you've tried this process yourself you do not discover something new about yourself or your past—or feel differently now about the complaint than when you began—continue inquiring into the complaint over the course of several days. Sometimes it can take as long as a month to get through the defenses to the layer of essence below, but when you get through you will know it. It will feel as though you have emerged from a dark, cramped, and airless passageway into an open space, filled with light and fresh air. Your heart will feel full, your mind clear and your body at peace.

Peeling Back the Layers

As we free ourselves from the tendency toward self-indulgence and cultivate healthy self-involvement, we gain the confidence to move beyond our defended personalities and toward our essential self. Instead of reacting with anger, dejection, or resistance when our partners say or do something we find disturbing, we can surpass the limits of our personalities by inquiring into our own reactions. This will bring peace or joy or love—whatever the quality we most desire—into the immediate situation. Knowing that there is more to us than patterns of behavior greatly accelerates the process of loosening and dissolving the more rigid aspects of our personality structure. We can challenge ourselves to come out of hiding behind the walls of our compensatory fortresses and risk exposure. We can be open, vulnerable, present, and awake.

Peeling back the layers is much like the process of a snake shedding its skin over and over again. As the essential part of us is allowed more space—through healthy self-involvement—we experience a corresponding shedding of outer layers of personality. As each layer of our defended personalities is peeled away and dissolved, we become more flexible and less reactive to life's circumstances.

This process of self-discovery has nothing to do with safety, comfort, or control—which are goals of personality-centered relationships. To the contrary, we purposely put our self-concepts and personal views at risk to know ourselves below our conditioned personalities. In this intimate way of relating, we strive for self-realization, not self-preservation—realization of our essential self, not preservation of our defended identity. In the service of authentic self-expression, we take full responsibility for our behavior, patterns, reactions and beliefs. We stretch ourselves so that we are uncertain as to what we will discover in the process.

Sometimes peeling back our defenses will be difficult. At other times, aspects of our personality will fall away of their own accord. However it happens, we can rest assured that the personality's defensive functions will not expire until we are ready to handle life and relationship without them. The idea of living without our old dependable, though often unsatisfying, ways of protecting ourselves can be frightening. We aren't used to functioning from an undefended place and initially can be terrified of our vulnerability. It is helpful to remember that our emotional defense structure is not fragile and will not give way prematurely or easily.

At the point that we connect with the full beauty and majesty of our essential self, we have the capacity to be present to ourselves and emotionally available to our partners. We are firmly rooted in the experience of ourselves as expansive, openhearted, strong, and loving, and fully capable of responding to every situation flexibly, appropriately, and compassionately. The fulfillment of our yearning to know ourselves then becomes the path to loving our partners without limitations or barriers.

CHAPTER 7

Moving Beyond the Impulse to REACT

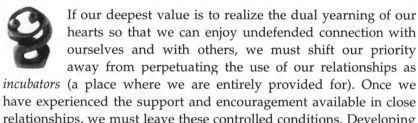 If our deepest value is to realize the dual yearning of our hearts so that we can enjoy undefended connection with ourselves and with others, we must shift our priority away from perpetuating the use of our relationships as *incubators* (a place where we are entirely provided for). Once we have experienced the support and encouragement available in close relationships, we must leave these controlled conditions. Developing intimacy requires that we find the courage to surpass the security and stability of our personality-centered strategies. We must, in fact, put at risk the level of closeness (or separateness) we have achieved thus far in our journey.

Even at healthier levels of connection, when we have greater resilience and flexibility in accommodating our partners' needs and tending to our own, we often continue to make choices to maintain emotional stability and security. As we have seen, the safety established in this way helps us see through our cracked identities; it provides the external support we need to regain access to our essential self. Prolonged emotional safety, however, can begin to feel like a straitjacket.

Remember—you have the support you need inside of you. You can create a nurturing holding environment for yourself when necessary. There are capacities, many essential qualities, that will be there when you need them. As you begin to experience more of this inner support, do not linger. You must proceed toward undefended intimacy.

We seldom feel ready to take this next step in our development. We cling to our old ways of maintaining emotional safety or closeness far longer than is necessary. Like the mother eagle who will dismantle the nest if her timid and scared eaglet resists taking flight, we must consciously dismantle our "nests" so that we may know the liberation of undefended love.

This chapter describes five conditions that define the apex of personality-centered relating and that prevent our movement to intimate relating if maintained too long or too adamantly. Although these conditions are appropriate for fostering genuine closeness and provide a supportive environment for cultivating healthy self-involvement, enforcing them as the primary objectives of a relationship limits our potential for unmediated contact. The paradox is this: All of these conditions operate naturally in an undefended partnership, emerging as by-products of the relationship rather than maintained as a its primary goals. But first we must endure the ordeal that is created as we release the footholds we have relied upon to keep us safe from emotional harm.

The five conditions that produce and reinforce the most developed levels of personality-centered relationships spell out the word REACT. Our clients find this acronym useful in helping them remember the conditions that prolong closeness while impeding intimacy. Every time we REACT, we are replaying an old script, often from unresolved issues dating back to our families of origin. Requiring that our partners behave in a certain way and defending ourselves when we feel threatened are basically REACTions to our past. The REACT acronym stands for:

1. **Reciprocity:** The expectation of fairness, equality, and an equal give-and-take.

2. **Entitlement:** The expectation of external confirmation that we are deserving.

3. **Approval:** The expectation of mutual acceptance and validation.

4. **Consensus:** The basic agreement in views about self and the world.

5. Trustworthiness: The ability to trust and depend on our partners.

On the surface, these conditions appear to be desirable in a relationship. They seem downright enlightened when compared to what most of our parents and grandparents expected in their marriages. However, like stepping-stones, they are meant to take us beyond the need for external supports that keep us feeling safe and in control. To achieve the capacity for undefended love, we must consciously choose to relax our reliance on these conditions.

According to Jean Klein (1984), a reaction is "a nonaccomplished action. . . . The residue of this nonaccomplishment remains in you as memory." On the other hand, he points out: "Spontaneous action is not related to memory and leaves no residue." Reactions reveal our relationship with our past, taking us away from the present moment. The spontaneity and freedom of action that characterize undefended relationships results from of our ability to be in the present—the "right here, right now"—as it is instead of reacting against it. This is the shift we undertake as we examine and release each of the five conditions that cement personality-centered relationships.

Reciprocity

I want to hear your part in the problem before
I am going to expose any more of my part.

—Rhonda, trial attorney from San Francisco

The capacity to relate *reciprocally* is one of the hallmarks of the highest level of personality-centered relationships. Both partners have concern for their own as well as each other's needs and wishes. Both are interested in equality, fairness, and maintaining the balance of power through give-and-take. Although a couple's ability to establish reciprocity is a positive sign of emotional maturity, it remains a bargaining mode of relating, best defined as, "I will if you will."

In other words, in some way we obligate our partners to give back. Whether our exchanges are made "in kind" or vary in form and nature, we believe they must be of equal value. If we disclose something of significance, we expect our partners to disclose something of equal importance. If we give something of value, we expect our partners to return something comparable. Every emotional exchange is somewhat conditional upon keeping the scales even. If one partner begins to have too much power, or is giving or taking too much, the rule of reciprocity is invoked and balance once again established. There is an implied threat, even if not consciously or explicitly acknowledged, that if the offending partner does not comply, something serious will happen.

When the balance of power is more important than knowing ourselves and each other at ever-deepening levels, we end up emphasizing the objects that are exchanged over relating openly with ourselves and each other. Instead of being forthcoming and vulnerable, we hold information back as collateral. When reciprocity is used to guarantee that we won't reveal more of ourselves than our partners do of themselves, our self-disclosures are less a pathway to discovery than a manipulation to control our level of vulnerability.

When preoccupied with personal protection, the relevance of each partner's experience becomes less important than maintaining the emotional status quo in the relationship. We strive to solve our problems and resolve conflicts through negotiation, even if it means curtailing someone's personal growth to do so.

Those of us who insist upon reciprocity in relationships are usually reacting to an inner experience of powerlessness or unresolved feelings about "not being given to." In our efforts to avoid facing and dealing with the heartache, fear, and rejection we felt in the past when we did not receive what we needed, we establish a protective pattern of balancing what we give with what we receive now.

We make sure we don't offer more than we receive. At face value this may appear to be self-protective in a responsible way. But there is a hidden cost. When we insist on reciprocity, *we define who we are in response to who another is*. We give only as much as our partners do and demand that they give what we expect. Forcing an equal give-and-take delays our ability to see what is truly available for us in the relationship—so we can make a conscious choice about whether the partnership is viable—and delays the development of authentic generosity and openheartedness, the qualities for which we yearn.

Committing to Unilateral Self-Exploration and Disclosure

Developing intimacy means relaxing the demand that our partners reciprocate. Instead, we substitute our own uncompromising commitment to unilateral self-exploration and disclosure. David Schnarch (1991), author and director of the Marriage and Family Health Center in Evergreen, Colorado, similarly comments, "A couple in which at least one partner is capable of sustained unilateral disclosure is more likely to successfully weather the missed opportunities and poorly phrased responses that often accompany . . . building a relationship." Schnarch goes one step further with the following promise: "It is in the struggle to maintain oneself unilaterally in marriage that the final resolution of childhood occurs."

This is challenging indeed. If our partners aren't reciprocating, our minds and hearts want to react with such notions as "It isn't fair!" The truth is, it *isn't* fair. Our capacity for undefended contact, however, is developed only when we can shift our focus away from maintaining a balance of power, and give our undivided attention to personal inquiry and responsibility. The results may not be immediately apparent, but, in time, we not only deepen our capacity to relate fully, we free ourselves from our bondage to the past and from needing others to relate to us in a certain way in the present. Instead of trying to balance the power between us, we achieve an inner sense of balance and stability.

Rather than use our energy to maintain reciprocity, an uncompromising commitment to unilateral self-exploration and disclosure frees us to examine the underlying need for reciprocity itself. When we explore our fear of being taken advantage of or feeling helpless, we see that the only authentic power resides in making peace within ourselves. No longer depending on our partners to behave in a way that maintains the status quo, we find that our sense of safety is grounded in our own ability to respond openly and fearlessly to any feelings that may rise in us. When we can emotionally "stand on our own two feet," intact, without reference to what our partners are doing or giving, we are finally able to relate to them as they are, not as we require or wish them to be. Only then can we objectively measure what is available in our relationship and whether it is satisfactory.

Once we remove the illusion of protection offered by the requirement for reciprocity, we find that we no longer experience a need for fairness or equality. Our self-exploration becomes an intimate form of self-expression and celebration; we invite our partners to do the same, but our behavior is not bound by their ability or willingness to do so.

Entitlement

*She has a constant sense of entitlement to more
than she could ever get.*

—Steven, a contractor from Texas

Many of us who bear childhood wounds of neglect have worked hard to develop a healthy sense that we are "deserving." This is the adult version of "I get to have." Without the sense that we deserve to receive, we do not explore our needs and wants, and we do not learn to give them expression. Knowing our needs and expressing them are important developmental achievements that support our journey to satisfying levels of closeness.

When we feel unsure that we are deserving—challenged by a cracked identity that has us believing we are unworthy or unlovable—we sometimes try to force or imitate a sense of being deserving before we actually know and feel it deeply inside us. This often manifests itself as a rigid sense of *entitlement*. That is, we believe that what we want is due or owed to us in some way, that it is our "right" to get it, and we have little tolerance for not receiving what we want or feel we need.

The quickest way to test the flexibility of our sense of entitlement is to imagine our partners refusing to give us something we feel we should receive. If we become self-righteous, hostile, feel victimized, or experience self-doubt, this indicates that we are trying to feel deserving. When our partners do not fill our needs, we conclude that it is a comment on whether we deserve to get what we want. As a result, we look to and require our partners to fill our needs and confirm the fact that we are deserving.

There is a Zen proverb that says, "When a pickpocket meets the Buddha, he sees only his pockets." When we try to compensate for our emotional pain of feeling undeserving by requiring our partners to confirm our sense of entitlement, we are more in relationship with trying to get something than we are in relationship with our partners. We become emotional pickpockets. In contrast, when we are firmly rooted in our own personal value, our certainty that we are deserving remains unaffected whether or not we receive what we want. We are openhearted and openhanded.

As members of a panel speaking about entitlement to a small group of men and women who experienced emotional neglect as children, Marlena and I had an excellent opportunity to explore the complexity of this issue with people struggling to deepen their understanding of it. We were struck by the depth of emotional pain these men and women experienced by not knowing what they deserve, what they should be allowed to have, and whether it was all right for them to have anything at all.

One older man caught our attention as he alternated between a somewhat hostile pronouncement of his entitlement and a collapsing sense of confusion, not knowing if what he was saying was at all "reasonable." He couldn't seem to find a comfortable position in his chair as he explained his inner turmoil: "If I assert my 'rights' I feel selfish, arrogant, disrespectful, and ungrateful. If I don't assert myself, I feel ripped off, punished, like I have no rights or have not been given my 'due.' This turns into self-hatred and self-loathing." When this kind of dilemma is played out in a relationship, no wonder interactions become confusing, without a satisfying or long-lasting resolution.

When we receive what we feel entitled to, we keep our emotional pain at bay. But as long as our sense of entitlement is founded in lack (our cracked identity), we can never get enough. Essentially, we are stuck in a defended, personality-centered dilemma. We are trying to *get* enough to remember that we *are* enough. We interpret "getting" as an indicator of whether or not we are loved. We interpret "not getting" as proof that we are indeed unworthy. Unable to bear the pain of that belief, we accuse our partners of being unwilling or unable to provide us with what we are entitled to. At the core of entitlement is mistrust of ourselves. That is, we believe that we are incapable of providing for ourselves.

The truth is, we are entitled to want and need. We are not, however, entitled to have the universe (or our partners) provide what we want and need. When we can let go of requiring our partners to give us what we think we deserve, we begin to see what is right before us, what the present moment is offering—we become more full of our own presence. This by itself is exhilarating and enlivening. Our demand that our needs be fulfilled is transformed into appreciation and gratitude. The way is open to undefended intimacy with ourselves and our partners.

Approval

I feel devastated when I can't get a constant stream of validation.

—Warren, journalist and novelist

I realize the subtext to everything I do for him is: "Am I doing it right?" "Are you happy with me?" "Is there anything else you desire?"

—Patricia, mother of three

To be able to give and receive *approval* is an important capacity in the early stages of personality-centered relationship. Many of us have felt so wounded by the lack of positive reflection and regard that having a sufficient amount of external approval is vital until we are firmly rooted in our intrinsic goodness. However, when we become attached to an external source of confirmation, we fail to make the transition to our own self-acceptance. As we shift our center of gravity toward essence-centered relating, it is important to use the positive reflections we receive as stepping-stones to finding the source of approval within.

Underlying the requirement that our partners make us feel acceptable is the fear that we are deficient or inadequate. Something is missing, and we seek to cover over that "flaw" with external approval. Unfortunately, covering up a hole does not fill it.

Many couples intent on providing and receiving complimentary attention have inadvertently created mutual admiration societies of their relationships. Instead of using positive reinforcement as support while they develop the capacity to access their own inner value, each becomes increasingly reliant on the other's positive mirroring.

Brian and Tony: Applying the Undefended Approach

Mutual approval worked well for Brian and Tony, a couple from Ohio. It was widely agreed that they had a model relationship. Equally supportive and approving, they set an example in their circle of friends for what closeness looks like. Tony was attentive to Brian's need for encouragement to try new things, helping Brian overcome a lifelong pattern of procrastination rooted in his fear of failure. Brian, in turn, consistently told Tony that he found him to be handsome, helping Tony overcome his belief that he is physically plain-looking.

In the early years of their relationship, this couple had recognized that they both needed a lot of positive reinforcement to heal old emotional injuries. However, their reliance on mutual approval continued longer than was beneficial. In the absence of their conscious choice to grow, life orchestrated, as it generally will, the circumstances that guided them to their next stage of development.

Brian lost his job as a market researcher. As months passed without success of finding another job, he began to feel lethargic and immobile. "I started to lose my sense of identity and then sank into a deep depression. I couldn't get out of bed in the morning and got really mad when Tony wasn't understanding about how hard things were for me."

Besides working full-time, Tony began to feel the strain of supporting his own and Brian's needs for positive attention. Because they both conceived of approval as something to be gained from an external source, it was only a matter of time before one of them would look outside the relationship. A coworker in Tony's consulting firm began to be very attentive to him. In an attempt to escape the influence of Brian's "vacant stares" and "out-of-work depression blues," Tony felt himself drawn more and more toward his coworker, eventually having a brief affair while away at a sales convention. "I was feeling down and unsupported. This guy was showering me with attention. I just wanted to feel good again—good about myself."

Tony and Brian came very close to breaking up over this incident, but luckily, in this case, financial circumstances (including the recent purchase of a home in a downward spiraling real estate market), prevented them from taking the easy way out. Forced to stop and examine what had happened, they realized that they had required approval from each other to such a degree that they could not sustain themselves in its absence.

As long as their lives were running smoothly, their ability to be mutually approving was not threatened. But most couples will, at one time or another, come to a crossroads where the relationship will be challenged to grow beyond what it has accomplished thus far. For Brian and Tony, these crossroads came in the form of facing a time when neither could put his personal needs on hold for the benefit of the other. In the past, one of them would muster up the energy to be encouraging and supportive of the other, but on this occasion, both Tony and Brian felt equally depleted and discouraged. For Brian, looking for a new job forced him to face his worst fear of taking risks and venturing out in the world anew. Confronting this daunting task, he was not able to bolster Tony's self-esteem. In the absence of Brian's reassurance, Tony looked elsewhere for support about his physical appearance.

Now, a number of years later, they have a much stronger and deeper connection that they report as more satisfying and less emotionally defended. Compelled to navigate this treacherous stretch in their relationship, they developed a way of relating that they had not attained in their mutual admiration society. "Dealing with the affair made us both realize that we had narrowed down our relationship to feel safe," Brian told us. "Even though it was painful to work through, the fact that we stuck in there with each other somehow means more to me than all the encouragement during the good times. This is the first time I really feel like I can depend on Tony, like we're in this together." Tony felt the same way: "I still can't believe I had the affair but now that I have, I can see how I have relied on Brian in ways that weren't clear to me before. I used Brian's attention to help me avoid the truth that I don't like myself very much. Somehow seeing this, I feel like I can do something about it."

When the external flow of positive regard is unavailable and we are pressed to face the negative self-concepts that get stimulated in its absence, we have the opportunity to use the situation to our advantage. Instead of demanding the approval we seek, we must willingly turn our attention toward the more permanently liberating work of recovering access to our intrinsic sense of value. The resulting self-acceptance is not contingent on an outside view to prop up our fragile sense of self. No longer requiring our partners to shower us with their positive regard, we can meet them intimately and lovingly.

Consensus

When there is a difference of opinion and we can't reach an agreement, I collapse. I just give up.

> —Debbie, marketing vice president of a software company

To acknowledge and accept your experience, I must devalue my own or leave the relationship.

> —Louis, graduate student at Ohio State University

The capacity to be in harmony or "of like mind" with our partners is important in building the kind of closeness that supports the healing of our cracked identities. In this way, the ability to reach *consensus* is a necessary prerequisite in the early development of a stable bond. It requires a sense of openness to another's point of view as well as a stretching of one's own internal map to include another's. This flexibility of consciousness creates a neutral common ground from which a couple can have a shared experience of themselves and the world. Once we are capable of reaching a good enough level of agreement with our partners to create a bond of closeness, we are ready to move to the next stage of learning to experience deeper levels of ourselves in the absence of that umbilical cord.

Needing consensus is often a way to mask unresolved feelings that are part of the initial experience of separation that occurred in the womb, during infancy, or in early childhood. Holding the same reality as our partners helps us to merge with them. When consensus is not possible, we face the anxiety of separation. By creating a shared reality, a shared truth with our partners, we avoid exposing ourselves to those distressful childhood feelings of anxiety or isolation. Striving to maintain consensus helps us avoid feeling empty and alone.

When we complain that we want improved communication, that we want to be understood, seen and heard, we often discover that what we really want is for our partners to agree with us—to see things in the same way we do. We are trying to reach consensus—a matching view of reality—and when we can't, we experience high levels of frustration or anxiety.

Some of us carry a deep pain about not feeling "right" or "valid" in our perceptions, needs, and feelings. Rather than addressing this inner conflict directly, we have been taught to seek agreement from others to validate or sustain our own internal reality. Thus we rely on our partners to agree with us so that we will feel secure enough to allow our view to unfold. What happens when we don't see things in the same way? Even if we intellectually grasp the concept that perception, reality, and truth are relative to our orientation to the world, in relationship we often hold an underlying belief that if we have divergent experiences, we must either give up our point of view or reject our partner's so as not to face the discrepancy. Instead of authentic accord, this attitude is intolerant of a separate or contradictory reality.

When we lose ourselves in relationship what's really happening is that we cannot know our own experience of ourselves in the presence of a significant other. We may feel responsible for our partners' pain or feel guilty when our experiences do not match. We may feel as if we don't exist if our partners hold a contrary view. We then require consensus to solve the problems in our relationship and need to be apart to know and express our unique point of view.

The capacity to sustain our view of reality in the face of a divergent one while remaining in relationship until an organic resolution is reached is one of the cornerstones of an undefended partnership. Sustaining our own view is not the same as rigidly defending our position as "right." It is a mature capacity to investigate both points of view with equal vigor and dedication, with the realization that there is a third more encompassing reality yet to be known.

By learning to face and tolerate the initial rush of difficult emotions when we cannot reach consensus with our partners, we develop a secure sense of self that does not depend on agreement with another. We no longer rely on defenses or conditions to prop us up or make us feel whole. If we are in touch with our essential self, when our partners express a reality different from our own, we are able to sustain a sense of ourselves as intact while remaining open to their point of view. Ultimately, we discover that our essential self is not really separate from our partner's, even though it is not identical.

Trustworthiness

I am always waiting for the other shoe to drop or scanning the environment for a potential disaster.

—Ed, television producer and single parent

If she isn't "catastrophizing" and "awfulizing," she is suspicious and mistrusting.

—Anne, civil engineer from Florida

When you *trust* your partner, what do you expect him to do for you? Perhaps you count on him to take care of you, be kind and loving, tell you the truth, protect you, be there for you, hold you, look out for you, or heal you. These are all answers from participants in our groups when asked this question.

When we look for trust in our relationships, we are generally concerned with issues of dependability, predictability, and consistency. We want to trust that what we expect to happen will happen. We trust that our partners will remain faithful; that they will do what they say they will do; that they will keep their agreements; that they will take care of us. There is nothing wrong with striving for or wanting this confidence to be present in our relationships. In the earlier developmental stages of relationship, this kind of trust is a necessary condition for healthy closeness. It is important to recognize, however, that when we require and demand trust and dependability in certain areas of a relationship as a way to feel safe and at ease, we are asking our partners to take responsibility for protecting our feelings. We are placing our feelings in their care.

Instead of simply trusting in our partners, we tend to "entrust" ourselves to them. This stage of primal trust, that every infant rightfully needs and relies on, is keynoted by the simple equation, "If you love me, you won't hurt me." Most of us know what happens when we hold that expectation too concretely and for too long into our adult relationships. Allie, a soft-spoken and kind woman in her late thirties, related that she had entered a relationship with "blind trust." Hoping everything would work out fine, in the name of trust she had swept a lot of issues under the rug. Of course, the relationship disintegrated in a relatively short period of time. Allie came to realize that her version of trust had been similar to blindfolding herself and trying to cross a busy freeway, all the while expecting nobody to hit her. We take refuge in this kind of blind trust because it is easy and comfortable; it allows us to hide from the truth, which is often complex and uncomfortable.

This primal stage of trust is too binding; if left unchallenged, it will block the fullness of conscious development. Life is intricate and perplexing—sometimes vast and chaotic. The more narrow and limited our understanding and expectations, the more we will feel betrayed by its paradoxes. Life is big. Many different circumstances can occur. The idea that everything will happen according to our preferences is unrealistic and a setup for disaster.

Within trust is embedded the possibility of betrayal. And it is in the context of a trusted relationship that trust is made and trust is shattered. When we feel outraged, shocked, or disillusioned in response to this fractured trust, we are being shaken out of a narrow resting place. The initiation leads us to discover our capacity to meet the fullness and complexity of the human condition. We only begin to grow once we stop clinging to our demand that life function the way we want it to.

Our insistence on trust in relationship can mask the fears of our cracked identities. To avoid these we trust that our partners will reflect back to us only the parts of us that we want to see. We trust that our partners will not confront us about our behaviors or beliefs. Any other response is seen as a radical betrayal because we believe that our partners would not evoke uncomfortable feelings in us if they loved us.

As we mature in relationship and desire more intimate levels of connecting, it becomes necessary to learn to rely on our faith in facing life with our eyes open. We replace the demand on our partners to be trustworthy with our own commitment to be available to the truth. We develop a faith in our capacity to say and hear the truth and to respond to it in an open and undefended way. We place our love of truth above our attachment to safety, comfort, and control.

In so doing, we surpass the objectives of personality-centered relating. Rather than entrusting another to protect our feelings because we cannot tolerate them, we trust our capacity to meet whatever arises. This wider context of awareness that includes the whole truth of what is occurring, not just the part that makes us feel safe and comfortable, enables us to respond to the ever-deepening reality that appears in front of us as we become increasingly less defended.

Meeting Our Partners Undefended

These five conditions—reciprocity, entitlement, approval, consensus, and trustworthiness—maintain personality-centered relationships by helping us avoid feeling vulnerable, exposed, overpowered, or rejected. At their core, all of these so-called "negative" feelings come from the experience of inner deficiency that characterizes our cracked identities. These conditions provide the context for the closeness we need as we learn to face our disappointments and fears directly and cultivate the inner resources that allow us to move into more intimate, subtle, and complex realms of relationship. As we release our attachment to each condition, we eventually experience the liberation, joy, and spontaneity of unconditional love. No longer requiring favorable conditions, we are free to meet each other fully and wholly, without defense or fear.

CHAPTER 8

Relaxing the Need to Have Our Needs Met

As we begin to relax the demand that our partners act strictly in accordance with the five conditions that maintain closeness, we discover an underlying urgency or inner hunger that may be described as a deep sense of need. This increased experience of neediness can result in a full range of uncomfortable feelings: We may feel anxious or desperate, frustrated, angry, victimized, or depressed. Once we understand the important role needs play in permanently surpassing the conditional love of personality-centered relationships, our impulse to feel "better" will be replaced by a commitment to feel "more."

To some degree, most of us believe that the measure of a good relationship is that it "meets our needs." As we have seen, this can reduce our partnerships to the level of trying to get needs met instead of connecting at ever-deepening levels. Learning to tolerate the flood of emotions that follow when we do not get what we need turns our attention toward the essential qualities that lie dormant in our being. If we are to reach our full potential for intimacy in relationship, we must relax our need to have our needs met.

In the course of a lifetime, our experience of needing goes through distinct developmental stages. If one or more of these stages was not completed—that is, if certain needs were not met at important times in our lives—we can, as we have seen, find ourselves endlessly pursuing these needs in our adult relationships. When we learn to harness the power of knowing our needs, instead of compulsively trying to satisfy them, we can move from dependency to healthy closeness and beyond to undefended intimacy. This chapter delves into the origins of emotional needs to see how they mature in successive stages.

The Developmental Progression of Needs

As infants we are entirely dependent on our environment to provide for our needs. Because we are essentially helpless, the experience of need carries a high level of urgency. We are our needs, and although emotional needs are important, they are subsumed by the absolute necessity for the physical body to stay alive. If a one-week-old infant is not fed within minutes of his experience of hunger, he has no internal buffer to sustain him. He experiences imminent danger to his survival and will appropriately raise a commotion to attract a response. If his physical need is not satisfied in a timely way, his emotional health is also impaired.

As the child matures, he develops the capacity to experience certain needs without demanding immediate gratification. He can tolerate moments of hunger, endure lack of rest, and deal with some delay of immediate response from the environment. A child in a supportive environment—one that is "feeding" him physically, emotionally, and psychologically—is learning healthy ways to sustain himself through frustrations of his needs on those levels as well.

Needs are natural and, in a healthy context, as the child matures into adulthood, he is less driven by them. The emotionally healthy adult recognizes that options and choices exist and thus is resilient in response to life's challenges. In the healthy development of the emotions—which results in a transparent personality—needs unfold in a natural progression.

The Continuum of Emotional Needs

We have all experienced the feeling of needing emotional support or recognition and knowing how little tolerance we have when we do not receive it. We also know what it is like to feel at peace whether or not we get emotional support or recognition, having no preference about it. These are the two poles of the Continuum of Emotional Needs.

The Continuum of Emotional Needs

Need———»Want———» Desire———» Preference———» No Preference

In the healthy process of maturing, we would move from compulsion about determining and controlling how we get our needs met to increasing levels of acceptance of what life offers us as sufficient. As enlightened masters demonstrate, at the most evolved level we do not need things to be other than they are—we have no preference. Everything carries equal value. This continuum also reflects what happens as we move from close relationship to the deep fulfillment of an undefended and unrehearsed partnership.

This natural and healthy development of our emotions typically was interrupted, however, because few of us escaped childhood without a certain amount of fear and pain connected with our experience of needing, physically and emotionally. Thus, we now experience our current emotional needs with the same level of urgency as we did those critical physical needs that threatened our survival. Just as the one-week-old infant screams and cries when he is hungry, we "scream" on an emotional level when we think our needs will not be met. We have all had the experience of feeling an intense reaction when a simple request we make to a significant other is not responded to satisfactorily. The frustration of our needs triggers a survival reflex that is linked with the utter vulnerability and helplessness we felt as infants and children.

These reflexive reactions hold important clues. The more charged and urgent they are, the earlier in our childhood are their points of origin. The earlier the unresolved need, the less capable we are as adults of sustaining our sense of well-being when that need is not fulfilled by another. To liberate ourselves from the grip of our unresolved past we must learn to investigate our needs, not satisfy them. In this way our needs serve to guide us to our essential self and those aspects we mistakenly believe are missing in us.

Allowing Ourselves to Need

If we are to move beyond our emotional infancy, we must first allow ourselves to explore what it feels like to need. For some of us, the emotional pain and fear we experienced when our needs were not met as children were so overwhelming that we eventually denied the presence of needs altogether. In an unpublished seven-year research study conducted at our center with more than five hundred clients and retreat participants, 33 percent of the respondents reported having lost the ability to identify and express what they need. Inviting the experience of need back into our lives is necessary to initiate this developmental process.

Les and Kate: Applying the Undefended Approach

Les, an office manager working for a midsize design engineering company, came to us for help. His wife had recently become more insistent that he "show up" in the relationship, refusing to tell him what she needed until he expressed what he needed first. "At first, I was relieved," Les explained. "I've always felt overwhelmed by—yet secretly admiring of—Kate's capacity to need so much, and in awe of her ability to ask me to meet her needs. But I was also indignant that she thinks she knows something more about my needs than I do. How dare she suggest that I'm shut down!"

As the weeks rolled by in a stalemate—Kate silently waiting for Les to come forward with what he needed and Les not feeling much of anything except resistance—Les began to comprehend the extent of the problem. He had not only lost the ability to know what he needed, he had very little understanding of what he was feeling in general. "This really bummed me out. I guess that's kind of a feeling. I thought Kate was mean. That's a feeling too, isn't it?" Then it dawned on Les that Kate's complaint was true. "I realized that if I do experience a need, it only seems to come up in contrast to something Kate is feeling or needing. I can agree or disagree, but I don't offer much information by myself."

As Les explored the origins of his pattern of not needing, he talked about how he had experienced his father as "volatile." "Everyone had to attend to him. We walked around on eggshells, hoping he wouldn't start drinking again. I can't even remember thinking it was possible to get anything—anything I wanted, that is—so I guess I shut down my own needs to avoid feeling disappointment."

Les knew that it would not be easy to allow himself to need again. He understood that once he did, the process was likely to trigger old losses, hurts, and resentment. But he was willing to endure the pain if he could begin to feel again. "I want to know what's going on inside of me. Right now I feel like I'm hollow—like I'm a shell of a person. I don't want to use Kate to fill up my world anymore."

Following our advice, Les began by setting his watch alarm to remind him to stop whatever he was doing for five minutes every hour. When he heard the beep, he listed all sensations and feelings he could perceive. He also began and ended his day by making such a list. "At first I didn't feel much at all. Then I began to feel angry that nothing was happening and realized that was at least a start." We encouraged him to take long, slow breaths, deep in his belly, to help him turn his attention inward.

After about a month, he began asking himself, periodically throughout the day, what it was that he needed in that moment. "Usually the answer was 'nothing' or 'I don't know.' So I began listing everything I thought I might need. I did this in very simple ways. I'd ask myself if I was thirsty. If I wasn't sure, I'd drink some water and see if that told me anything. Over time, I began to feel some needs such as hunger, warmth, and reassurance. It was a lot like what I saw my father go through after his stroke. He had to relearn everything he had taken for granted but was no longer automatic."

Reconnecting with the experience of need was an essential step for Les. His next task would be to learn to use his needs as navigational tools to help him discover his own wholeness and fullness.

Those of us who did not shut down our needs may respond to them by compulsively trying to fill or distract ourselves from them. Either way, we are fixated at the level of need; we are in relationship with our needs, not ourselves or our partners. Once we recognize that fulfilling needs is only a temporary stop-gap, we are ready to suspend our compulsion to gratify them. At that point, we give ourselves the opportunity to "grow up" instead of "fill up." When we slow down our efforts to get what we think we need and, instead, turn our attention to inquiring more deeply into the internal experience that our needs bring up in us, we set foot on the path that will lead to the fulfillment of our deepest desires. If we remain consciously aware that we are afraid our needs may not be fulfilled, without attempting to push the fear away nor indulge in it, we begin to develop the courage that will support us in surviving our terror. Simply allowing ourselves to experience our needs enables us to develop the inner capacities that will allow intimacy to unfold.

Even though we may initially experience high levels of discomfort and anxiety when our needs are not met externally, we ultimately discover that "bad" feelings do pass and we can sustain ourselves through the transition. We begin to develop healthy ways of soothing ourselves in response to life's inevitable frustrations. Soothing ourselves is not about making ourselves feel more comfortable. It is about supporting ourselves through every experience. Here are the ways six clients have found to soothe themselves. As you read this list you might reflect on how you support yourself when in the midst of difficult feelings.

Dale: I take a walk and do my best not to change what's happening inside, while making sure I don't let my mind draw conclusions or make up stories to make myself feel better or worse about what's happening.

Annie: I focus on my breathing, taking long slow breaths and letting my feelings come and go in waves.

Mark: I hold myself, placing one hand on my heart and one on my belly, and remind myself that I'm OK.

Randy: I take a bath and let the experience have its way with me.

Cheryl: I draw what the feelings look like, trying to give them more space in my awareness.

Annette: I journal about the sensations and feelings, being attentive to resist the temptation to feel sorry for myself or panic about how this may affect my ability to function.

Developing the Capacity to Want

As we develop the inner support necessary to sustain ourselves through survival fears, the driven quality of our emotional needs matures into the freer capacity to "want." Once again, some of us may find that we have to reopen to the willingness to want, which might have been shut down when our wants were repeatedly denied or punished. Just as maturing through the stage of needing requires experiencing need rather than filling it, the challenge of the wanting stage is learning to sustain ourselves through the experience of wanting and not receiving.

For most of us, wanting is inextricably tied to "getting." In fact, more than a few clients have stared back at us in amazement when we have told them that wanting, without placing attention on getting, serves a vital developmental function. If we want something, we assume the only way to satisfy ourselves is to get it. However, it is possible to experience a deep sense of fulfillment and satisfaction by simply remaining attentive to the experience of wanting without rushing out to get. This surrendering of our attachment to getting is very different from "giving up," which happens when we either believe we are undeserving or we have collapsed in despair as a consequence of too many past disappointments.

If we simply remain with the experience of wanting—knowing it, expressing it, and relating to it fully—we find a different kind of satisfaction in the very process. Though this may be hard to grasp mentally, you can try it and see. Ask a trusted friend to spend a half hour with you as you allow yourself total freedom to just want. Lie down, set a timer, and begin listing (out loud) as many wants as you can, connecting deeply with each and allowing any feelings that arise to flow through you. You might want to have a fulfilling relationship, to love more deeply, to express your feelings with less censorship, or to work at a job where your contribution is appreciated. While engaging in this process, do not imagine getting or not getting what you want. Focus only on wanting itself. Express the want in one sentence, resisting the temptation to explain why you want it.

We find that when we facilitate this process with large groups of men and women, the transformation is remarkable. Almost everyone ends up smiling and calm. Instead of the palpable tension that existed at the beginning of the session, after just one half hour there is a feeling of contentment and peace in the room. Giving ourselves the freedom to want, with total presence, roots us deeply within ourselves. We are not split by the expectations, dissatisfactions, calculations, and frustrations we experience as we try to satisfy each want. When we can identify and accept our wants—without inhibitions or judgment—and allow our reactions to simply exist, we feel more space inside of us. All of our wants and associations with not getting dissolve and we feel full and light. Most people discover toward the completion of this process that they are less invested in filling their wants than when they began.

It is possible to bring this same process into our daily lives. As we allow ourselves to fully experience wanting—and further develop our capacity to sustain ourselves in the face of not receiving—we begin to direct ourselves toward the inner fullness we have overlooked.

The Generative Power of Desire

As the necessity or urgency to gratify our wants lessens and the capacity to sustain ourselves without external support increases, wanting matures into "desiring," which is slightly more detached from the imperative for immediate gratification that is characteristic of the earlier stages of needing and wanting. By the time we develop the capacity to desire, we have a greater ability to sustain ourselves without having to have what we desire.

The ability to feel desire is a critical leap from the prior stages. Whereas needing and wanting are, for the most part, reactions to something we feel is missing and necessary, desire is yearning for something because we have an interest in it and receptivity toward it.

When we begin to exercise our capacity to desire, our center of gravity shifts closer to the domain of essence, because desire is *generative*. It originates in us and from us, independent of what has been available or unavailable in our past. As with needing and wanting, when desires arise there is still some restriction or tension in us. But our experience is no longer tied to our survival or to the belief that we "have to have it or else."

Steve and Sarah: Applying the Undefended Approach

Steve is in a relationship that "works," and he has learned to experience, rather than act on, his neediness when it emerges. He feels competent at managing his emotions when he wants something that his partner, Sarah, is unwilling or incapable of providing.

Recently, however, Steve tells us he is noticing something else: an inner pull toward a deeper level of connection with Sarah. He describes this new sensation by telling us what it is not.

"It's not a need because I don't have the frenzied inner push to deal with it right away. It's not a want, because, again, I don't feel the same compelling urge to control it or manipulate to get it." He tells us it feels more relaxed, but not to the point of his ignoring it. Instead of an inner pressure he feels the "energetic support" to move toward what interests him.

What Steve is describing is desire. Desire has a sense of initiative without the push to mount a campaign or crusade to accomplish its end.

Experiencing Preferences

Desires, in turn, mature into preferences, in which a further degree of detachment—with no lessening in engagement—is evident. By the time we reach the stage where we are experiencing preferences rather than desires (or needs or wants), we are capable of living from essence more often than not. When we reach the preference stage we are only slightly concerned with having our preference acknowledged, and we feel little to no emotional pain if our preference is not fulfilled. We experience more freedom and flexibility in our response to what life brings us. Being less attached does not mean that we are not fully alive and interested. It simply means that we experience relative contentment and minimal inner conflict, restriction, or tension about whether our preference is satisfied or not.

The Freedom to Have No Preference

Over time we experience fewer and fewer preferences until we have "no preference" at all. At this point, we have shifted our center of gravity away from the defended personality and are firmly rooted in our essential self. When all experiences are valued equally, we no longer prefer one over another. We do not reject experiences we consider negative, nor do we overindulge in those we favor. Having no preferences does not mean that we are inactive, withdrawn, or indifferent. It means that we remain open, present, and available to all of life as it presents itself to us.

The *Xin-xin-ming*, presumed to have been written by the Sengcan (1999), Third Patriarch in the Chinese Zen lineage, is one of the earliest known works to recognize that every being has Buddhanature; that is, each of us can be enlightened. How? By cultivating the capacity for no preference. He writes: "The Great Way is not difficult for those who have no preferences. When love and hate are both absent, everything becomes clear and undisguised. Make the smallest distinction, however, and heaven and earth are set infinitely apart. If you wish to see the Truth, hold no opinions for or against anything. To set up what you like against what you dislike is the disease of the mind. When the deep meaning of things is not understood the mind's essential peace is disturbed to no avail."

Free from desires and preferences, we meet life wholeheartedly and experience ourselves as fresh, alive, and spontaneous. We are grateful for how things are, with no need, want, desire, or preference to have them be otherwise. Without preference, we discover that we have it all. This is the quality we possess when we are in a mature, intimate partnership.

The Incredible Power of Nonreactivity

To be objective—to be without a preference—we have to be nonreactive. We cannot be objective and reactive at the same time because reactivity is located in the past: We are "reactivating" the past. To be without preference we have to be in the present moment.

It's easy to tell when we are reactive. Here is the litmus test. How would you feel if someone said to you, "You are wearing a yellow shirt," when you are, in fact, wearing a blue one? You'd probably feel neutral or perhaps inquisitive about the person's perceptions. When someone says something about you and you feel anything other than neutral, you must explore the sensitivity in you that their comment stimulated. If you recall from chapter 3, your sensitivity is pointing out a broken toe that must be tended.

The method that will help you cultivate nonreactivity is this: If you usually yell, don't yell; if you generally try to get your partner to act in some different way, restrain that impulse; if your habit is to burst into tears, try holding them back; if you tend to become verbally demanding when your needs aren't being met, don't speak.

Do not underestimate the power of nonreactivity. What is most important about this practice, in terms of creating the capacity for undefended love, is where your attention goes when you react. When you yell your attention is pulled into the impulsive action. To do that you have to leave yourself—you abandon your own experience in the moment. This is the practice: Experience what happens when you simply do not do what you usually do. If you don't react, you get to retain your attention. In that instant of stopping, you open the possibility for a new experience.

The Treasure Waiting to Be Found

On our journey to undefended and unrehearsed connection, passing through each of the stages on the Continuum of Emotional Needs (need, want, desire, preference, no preference), we become progressively liberated from our reliance on external sources, ultimately realizing that the source of all fulfillment lies within us. Knowing that we can rely on ourselves, we no longer need our partners to give us whatever it is we thought would make us feel safe and valuable. Instead of requiring that our partners make us feel comfortable and loved, those who have shifted their center of gravity toward the domain of essence invite their relationship to reflect back all of the places where each is asleep, unconscious, and in conflict. Intimate partners share the understanding that relationships are meant to have tension and discomfort as they reveal to each other aspects that are difficult to tolerate. They appreciate this mirroring, recognizing its service as liberating them from the unresolved issues of the past and stimulating access to their own essential self.

Unfortunately, there is no easy formula that determines a successful passage from the seeming safety of personality-centered, controlled connection to the limitless opportunities of undefended intimacy. It is not entirely about getting needs met or neglecting ourselves, in the same way as it is not about always demanding reciprocity, entitlement, approval, consensus, and trust, or never requiring these conditions. How this passage happens will vary for each couple, depending upon the emotional depth and maturity each partner has developed.

What is true for all of us is that the movement beyond personality-centered relating requires some frustration of what we feel we need and want. It also requires that we struggle with the resulting emotional discomfort.

When we forego the safety and control of closeness and getting our needs met, we encounter the anxiety and discomfort that lead us to our deepest fears. Some of our clients describe the experience in dramatic terms: "I'd rather eat glass than feel this way." "When he's mad, I look at his face and feel a thousand doors slamming shut inside me." "I'd rather hit my head with a hammer than reveal something I know she'll react to. At least I know there's an end to the pain from the hammer." "I freeze in her presence and don't thaw out until I can be by myself." Yet these are the very experiences we must face if we wish to cultivate greater intimacy.

Unexpectedly, the source of fulfillment is revealed to have been present, within us, all along. "The beautiful thing about treasure is that it exists. It exists to be found," we are told by the Log Lady, soothsayer in the television series *Twin Peaks* (Lynch/Frost 1989).

"Where is the treasure that when found leaves one eternally happy? I think we all know it exists. Some say it is inside us. . . .That would be strange. It would be so near. Then why is it so hard to find and so difficult to attain?" The rewards of moving through the dis-comfort of relaxing our need to have our needs met—unrestrained joy, fathomless love, personal meaning, freedom, etc.—are well worth the emotional effort.

CHAPTER 9

What Do You Want—Finally?

As we go deeper into the challenging task of dissolving our defenses, we enter unfamiliar emotional terrain and it can become difficult to keep our bearings. We need a compass that can guide us, especially in the midst of a heated exchange or emotional meltdown. The qualities of our essential self can actually serve as that reliable compass. Paradoxically, these qualities are embedded in what seems to be the very root of our suffering—our needs and wants. Just as our needs can initiate our maturing toward "no preference," as we saw in chapter 8, so too can they become navigational aids in helping us find our essence.

In the chart of Personality Preoccupations and Strategies (see chapter 4) we saw that the needs and wants of each cracked identity correspond to qualities of our essential self. Although obscured by the internal tension and struggle we have carried since childhood, these qualities have been within us all along. Our relationships, therefore, cannot give us feelings of wholeness, peace, freedom, joy, love; they simply help us to recognize these essential qualities within ourselves by reflecting back to us aspects of ourselves that we do not see. We can then recover those aspects of ourselves that we believe we lost long ago when we began our process of individuation.

In the pursuit of our needs and wants we realize our deepest desire. In this chapter we will learn how our deepest desire can serve as a compass to guide us when we feel emotionally lost, alone, and without the strength to carry on. Identifying this desire provides us with a vision we can rely on in our passage beyond our current stage of relationship toward a liberating new way of relating that is without limitations.

Self-Inquiry: Following Your Needs Home

In chapter 4, we explored our preoccupations by identifying the three things we need or want most from our partners, for example: to be accepted, to be a priority in our partner's life, and to be respected. We recognized that what we most want is whatever we feel we need to keep our cracked identities intact—and thus remain emotionally secure. We found, too, that it is possible to simply experience our needs and wants rather than to feel compelled to satisfy them.

The following process will guide you toward your deepest desire, which will become the compass for the overall journey and an invaluable tool when you find yourself in the middle of a heated exchange or painful interaction with your partner. Once you have learned how to use this compass, even when you feel completely lost or disconnected, you will know how to stay focused on the realization that you already *are* what you seek.

Step One: Choosing What You Really Want:

Recall the three things you previously identified in chapter 4 as what you most need or want from your partner. Take a moment to feel again their deep importance to you, their meaning, and the urgency you feel about them especially when you are emotionally triggered. Recognize any discomfort or anxiety that is evoked in naming them.

Now, let's assume that in your lifetime you will only fulfill one of the three. Let's also assume that to be sure that this one will be satisfied, you must sacrifice the other two. Take a moment to let this sink in.

Out of your list, select one emotional need or want that you feel is the most important for you to realize in your lifetime. What do you want more than anything else in relationship? Which needs would you be willing to sacrifice for the fulfillment of the one?

You may experience anxiety or resistance to this process. You may fear that placing all your eggs in one basket will threaten your emotional survival. It is good to acknowledge this fear and resistance while trusting in the possibility of undefended love. Investigating what you are willing to risk everything for focuses you clearly and quickly on what is most important to you. Until we have grappled with this process, we will continue distracting ourselves with an infinite array of needs, wants, and personality-centered concerns.

John: Applying the Undefended Approach

When our client John set out to determine what he wanted most in relationship, he found himself confused. At first he thought he wanted his partner to be less depressed. Then it occurred to him that what he most wanted was to have more fun with his partner. This, in turn, led him to believe that he wanted to feel free to be himself in his relationship. But he also wanted more intimacy, connection, and contact. His need for freedom and the need for greater intimacy seemed to conflict with one another. How could he choose one over the other?

The more John inquired into this question, the more anxious and distressed he became. He didn't want to choose unless he could be certain that he would choose the "right one," the single most important thing he wanted. "I feel stuck," John said. "I can't make this choice." After struggling for a while, he realized that not choosing was a passive way of choosing.

As John reviewed his list, he discovered that his choices were a reaction to what he was currently experiencing; he was still not choosing what he truly wanted. His interest in intimacy was a reaction to his partner's recent signs of indifference in the relationship. His pull toward freedom was a result of his fear of being overwhelmed by what he saw as his partner's depression. As he began to allow himself to identify what he wants, not in reaction to what he wasn't getting or what he felt he should want, John came to a new and profound realization: He wanted to feel that his partner understood him.

As you review your own list, examine whether your choice is a reaction to current circumstances rather than an acknowledgment of what you want. The key to making this selection is understanding that this necessary choice will lead us home. Choosing is more about starting a journey that opens us to new possibilities than it is about leaving behind what we thought was needed to survive.

Step Two: Following Your Choice to Its Point Of Origin

Now that you have determined what you most want in relationship, you are ready to take the next step—following the thread of that need until it leads you back to your essential self, back to the qualities that are uniquely and utterly you. For instance, if the one choice for which you are willing to sacrifice all others is to be understood—as John identified his in the example above—use this as the starting point to probe deeper and deeper into that need, uncovering the layers of perceived loss that give rise to it.

Using this example, begin by asking yourself: If you were understood, what would that give you? Perhaps you would be free of the constant struggle to be heard and to feel accepted by your partner. You would no longer have to fight to feel acknowledged.

Now look below this need to what is motivating it. If you felt you were truly understood and no longer had to struggle to be heard, then what would you really have? Perhaps you would feel that you'd have more room to be yourself.

Once again, what is motivating this need? What would having more room to be yourself provide you? Perhaps you would feel more relaxed, in your body and in your mind. In that state of relaxation, how would you experience yourself? Perhaps you would feel calm, quiet, peaceful. Allow yourself to experience this peace.

The final question to ask yourself is: Are you willing to sacrifice all other needs and wants to know yourself as peace? At the point when you can genuinely answer yes to that question, you will experience a tremendous sense of relief. You no longer fear losing something by putting all your eggs in one basket. If you know yourself as Peace (or Strength, Joy, Love, or any other essential quality), all other needs are satisfied or dissolved, for this is the character of your essential self that has existed all along.

When we feel stuck, lost, or don't know how to get beyond an impasse with our partners, the first step is to stop trying to get them to give us what we want. We must follow, not fulfill, our needs and wants. We can then reconnect with our deepest desire instead of allowing ourselves to be pulled in many directions. In this way we come to the final realization that we already are what we seek.

Taking the Steps to What You Really Want

Begin your own process now by stating the one need you choose as most important for you in your relationship. What do you want more than anything else? Take several minutes to connect deeply with it. Feel the urgency behind it in your body by noticing any tension you may feel about expressing it or naming it. Feel any fear or anger that may surface from having wanted this for so long. Then begin asking yourself each question.

1. What do I want more than anything else in relationship?
   Example 1: I want someone who will accept me completely.
   Example 2: I want to feel loved.

2. If that desire were fulfilled, what would that give me?
   Example 1: Someone who would be there for me and with me.
   Example 2: It would give me an end to the questioning and self-judgment.

3. If I had that state/feeling/situation in my life, what would I really have?
   Example 1: I'd have the feeling of connection that I long for.
   Example 2: I'd feel OK about myself.

4. How would I feel to have that sense of myself? How would I experience myself differently than before?
   Example 1: I would feel happy and alive.
   Example 2: I would feel calm, without tension.

5. How would I describe this state of being (quality of essence)?
   Example 1: Joy.
   Example 2: Peace.

By the time you reach the fourth and fifth questions, you may experience a sense of relief. You might also find a quieting of your mind that makes it difficult to articulate your answers. The relaxation you feel is a clue that you have moved out of the domain of personality—leaving behind your habitual struggle to get what you feel you have lost—and are approaching your essential self and its rich qualities.

Even though the moment of living in your essential self will pass, this beginning plants the seed of a desire—whether for joy, love, peace, or any other essential quality—that will affirm your wish to live less defensively. Guided by this deepest desire, you will learn, over time, how to live in that instant of fulfillment regardless of circumstance—whether you are in the midst of a sweet, gentle embrace or triggered in an old, emotionally charged dynamic with your partner.

The teachings of Sufism, a mystical branch of Islam, distinguish between a *state* and a *station* to identify the difference between a passing experience and one that we abide in. A state is temporary; it has a beginning and an end—we get it and we lose it. In contrast, a station is an experience we can draw on whenever needed. If we have achieved the quality of joy as a station, we can tap into joy regardless of circumstances. We are all born with the potential to know ourselves as the full range of essential qualities. The work of dismantling our defenses allows us to realize these qualities as stations, knowing not only that they are in us, but that the resulting profound sense of belonging and wholeness can be experienced at all times.

Undefended intimates are committed to using the crucible of relationship to develop their capacity to express their essential qualities more of the time, ultimately using their love for one another to help them realize a deep and unwavering experience of their essential self.

Using Our Deepest Desire
As a Compass

Having identified our deepest desire for an essential quality that we wish to recover, we can examine every interaction in our relationships in light of the following question: Is what I am doing nourishing or distracting me from recovering that essential quality? This question acts as a compass to guide us when our course feels obstructed or unclear. When we know where we are headed, every action can be assessed: Is what we are doing moving us toward or away from our deepest desire? We may not, in every circumstance, be able to experience our essential qualities, but at least we will consciously know whether we are headed toward them in each case.

Julia: Applying the Undefended Approach

Julia, one of our clients, was trying to decide whether her partner, Ed, should move into her home. This possibility had been discussed many times in the course of their six-year relationship, but the couple had never been able to work through their fears and reactions about this increased level of commitment. Invariably one or the other would pull back from the relationship until the question appeared to go away. Then they would continue until the issue would mysteriously resurface again.

In the course of our work together, Julia embarked on the self-inquiry process to identify her deepest desire. Starting with the need of her personality to feel respected, she discovered her deepest desire to "know her own truth." After further exploration she realized that she had lost touch with her ability to know and speak her truth (for fear of the other's reaction) and, as a result, she found herself feeling "censored." Armed with her newly found conviction, Julia said it was now possible for her to endure the emotional discomfort she felt when disclosing what was true for her—anything would be better than feeling "silenced."

This personal desire to recover access to her own truth led to a new vision for her relationship: To know and express her deepest truths with Ed and to create an environment in which he felt invited to do the same. Clarifying this for herself did not eliminate the fears she had of living together, but it did give her a bigger context within which to view her ambivalence.

Once Julia understood the essential quality she was seeking—truth—she realized she could use the exploration of living together as a vehicle to bring her closer to what she most dearly desired. Now, instead of thinking she had to make the decision first and then discover later whether she could risk expressing her truth, she began to use every conversation about moving in together as a way to develop her capacity to do what she most deeply wanted. The focus was no longer on making a decision, but on discovering and expressing ever-deeper layers of her truth. She could also get a first-hand experience of how Ed would relate to being in a relationship with someone committed to telling him the truth, no matter how hard it was for her to say, or him to hear. Would he be able to listen to her without becoming defensive? Would he respond openly and truthfully?

In every conversation after that, Julia noticed what she was choosing to reveal and what she was choosing to conceal. Then she would ask herself, "When I stop telling him what I feel because I am afraid of his reaction, am I moving toward the capacity to know and tell the truth?" The answer clearly was "no."

It seems miraculous: When we maintain an unwavering attention on the essential quality we most desire, we are less invested in the need to control a situation and more committed to letting the impasse bring us to a deeper understanding.

A "happy resolution," which for Julia and Ed meant living together committed to the "truth," is not the sole measure of success. In other words, success doesn't mean staying together and failure doesn't mean ending the relationship. Even if the outcome had been separation, by identifying and living in accordance with her deepest desire, Julia had grown from being an uncertain woman who used ambivalence as a defense into a more confident and self-sustaining person, capable of exploring and expressing the truth as she knew it to her partner.

Our deepest desire offers a context within which our life can unfold. It is a container that helps us hold the larger picture. If we forget what we want, or we feel lost and confused, our deepest desire—our compass—will reliably take us home every time. If we feel overwhelmed or frightened, simply knowing that the emotional distress we are experiencing is in the service of achieving our heart's desire will give us the strength to endure. Now the same needs that tormented us for most of our lives become the supportive parent we never had. When followed, they remind us that it's time to come home to our essential self.

From Healing to Transformation

The more we experience our essence, and experience the joy and peace there, the more we are drawn to it as our base of relating. In this natural unfolding we begin to release our hold on the safety of closeness and move into the spontaneity of intimacy. As we have seen, the objective of personality-centered relating, when consciously undertaken, is to receive the necessary support that allows us to heal enough to move on to our next developmental step, undefended intimacy. The intention of this essence-centered way of relating is *transformation*.

Marlena clarified the distinction between healing and transformation by contrasting her experience of two friends. "When I talk to Morgan I feel a closeness, a kind of deep camaraderie in which I can share what's happening in my life, cry with her over the gains and losses, and talk about whatever is on my mind. It is a mutual sharing where we trade off, back and forth, and I feel understood and heard. In the warmth and welcoming of our connection, I feel restored and healed.

I have a different experience when I talk to Leigh. I feel stimulated. Our conversation guides me into the innermost center of my being. It's like a dance. Each of us ignites the other into further discoveries. It's not simply an open system like I feel with Morgan; it is a generative system that comes out of our contact. It's alchemical. As a result of our exchange, I uncover an unknown aspect of myself in the presence of someone else. I feel exposed and, in that exposure, transformed in some way."

Marlena's interaction with Morgan describes the experience of those operating from the healthiest levels of the domain of personality: They have a level of openness in which they are willing to express what they are feeling and what is happening in their lives. The contact depends upon certain agreements—in effect, the five conditions of reciprocity, entitlement, approval, consensus, and trustworthiness that were discussed in chapter 7—and the resulting closeness feels warm and safe.

What we have just described may look like intimacy to many people; however, real intimacy requires none of these conditions—although they may all be present. In fact, an undefended connection can feel very unsafe, out of our control, and quite uncomfortable. It is a metamorphic process in which we are not controlling the connection, but becoming absorbed by it and transformed through the contact. The intention is not simply to share our lives, but to peel back the many layers of life. We are not moving side by side, we are intermingling and intersecting each other's paths. Instead of exchanging stories we are unraveling them.

When we are undefended, our self-exposure occurs without the guarantee that we will be heard, seen, or accepted in the way we are in healthy closeness. At times, this level of intimacy can be so hot and scary it feels more like a shattering combustion than a safe, cozy exchange. At the same time, however, we experience ourselves in a heightened way, feeling very awake, alive, passionate, and vital and our contact has profound meaning and depth.

Although, for simplicity, these developmental stages are presented here in a linear fashion, keep in mind that as multidimensional beings, we are all operating on many levels simultaneously. Surpassing one stage of development does not mean that we no longer operate in the prior stages. Sometimes we will find ourselves relating at higher levels in one interaction only to plummet into a prior level when some unconscious pattern is triggered. Although the earlier stages preclude the later ones, undefended intimacy includes the capacity to experience *all* previous levels, including the highest level of closeness we have achieved.

Cultivating Butterfly Consciousness

It can be challenging for us to recognize relationship as a developmental process. When we have lived in one stage and learned it well, we can mistake it for the one and only reality. When we are ready to move on, the next challenge we face is expanding our vision of what is possible in relationship by recognizing that it is not just an extension of our present experience, but rather a leap beyond.

A cartoon published in *The New Yorker* magazine illustrates this predicament. In it, two caterpillars are looking up at a butterfly in a tree. One caterpillar turns to the other and says, "You'll never catch me up there!" Just as the caterpillar and the butterfly live in two very different environments, the experience of one stage of relating doesn't necessarily prepare us for the experience of the next. Without a clear vision of the way relationship would look without our usual defenses, we will, like the caterpillar, remain unconscious, resistant, or frightened of transformation.

Getting a sense of the bigger picture will support us through the inevitable discomfort of the passage. From a caterpillar's perspective, the cocoon is seen as a death chamber, whereas from the butterfly's perspective the cocoon is the passageway to birth and liberation. In the same way, when we feel dependent on our partners' approval, interrupting our personality's strategies to receive that approval will feel very uncomfortable. Once liberated from the need for external confirmation, we see how passage through our discomfort has freed us to know and love our partners and ourselves beyond any way of relating we had experienced before.

However, much as we might like to, we cannot simply bypass the challenges of our present stage of relationship. If all we have experienced with another is rigidity and brittleness, for example, we cannot suddenly create a relationship that is resilient and flexible. We must fully live out each stage of relationship.

When we are engaged in personality-centered relating, our movement from dependence to healthy closeness can be likened to the growth from larva to caterpillar. It is an extension of one form to another. The form of the larva is similar to the caterpillar, but the latter is bigger, more developed, and has greater mobility and independence.

The journey to intimacy calls for a radical shift in consciousness. This new reality cannot be extrapolated from our old ways of connecting; it is not an extension of where we find ourselves today. It is like the transformation from caterpillar to butterfly: The entire form changes, and the experience is one of dissolution and liberation. We cannot make this transition if we cling to caterpillar consciousness, requiring our partners to respond to us only in ways that make us feel comfortable. The extent to which we insist that our relationships provide for our personality needs is the extent to which we prolong our stay as caterpillars.

An undefended partnership cultivates butterfly consciousness. It recognizes that our relationships must frustrate the needs of our caterpillar selves—namely, the need to feel safe, in control, and without emotional pain. In so doing, we enter the process of transformation. In the cocoon, the caterpillar must let go entirely of its identity. There is a complete meltdown and restructuring of its components. Like the movement from caterpillar to butterfly, developing the capacity for undefended intimacy requires an internal *metamorphosis*, not a linear, step-by-step change. It is a leap of consciousness, a transformation of the entirety of our experience. This metamorphosis takes time—a lifetime—and happens, as we have seen, in stages.

Each developmental stage of relating prepares us for the next; we reside in one stage until we have developed a capacity to surpass it. But, unlike the butterfly, we have to actively challenge our previous form. As we learn to consciously use the tension and discomforts in our relationships for our personal growth, we begin to liberate ourselves from inaccurate and constricting beliefs about ourselves. If we are wise, we learn to see our partner's behaviors as invitations for us to realize and express the qualities of our essential self as we move through the developmental stages of relationship toward undefended love.

Then we can learn to spread our wings. And wings are precisely what we need, because we have come to the jumping-off place. Our journey beyond the limitations of personality can be compared to the belief in Christopher Columbus' day that the world was flat. When we come to the edge of one world view, we must step beyond everything we believe. We must step beyond the conditions that make us feel safe. We must step beyond our strategies and preoccupation to get our needs met. We must step beyond the impulse to defend, withdraw, or attack. Having the vision of what is possible and an infallible compass to guide us over the edge, we are ready to move into the deepest and most challenging part of the process—dissolving our defenses. For this is what it's all about: To live and love with an undefended heart.

CHAPTER 10

Dissolving Our Defenses

If we are to realize our potential to know ourselves as whole and loving, to express the open, present beings that we are, and to love ourselves and others from our undefended cores, we must turn and face all the places where we are stuck, wounded, withholding, and contracted. We must work directly with all that we fear, resist, vilify, disown, and reject. This includes our primitive or undeveloped aspects, negative self-images, emotional attachments, what we project as "other" and deny within ourselves, our self-doubt, judgment, greed, hostility, shame, confusion, and anything else that we consider negative or unpleasant.

It is in grappling with these "demons," rather than avoiding them, that we dissolve our shields. Undefended partners do not conspire to eliminate emotional pain and uncomfortable feelings. Instead, they are allied with each other in learning how to use whatever presents itself—unresolved losses, disappointments, dissatisfactions, needs, unworthiness, boredom, loneliness, depression, resentments, lust—in ways that allow them to reveal their essence to themselves and each other.

Embedded in the desire for intimacy is the understanding that our potential includes a wide range of experience, whose expression brings out the richness of all that is human. When we live within the comfort zone of our defended personalities, we confine our existence much in the way a pianist would be limited if the only key he could use was C. The journey to the heart of undefended intimacy is about regaining the use of our entire keyboard, not repetitively banging out our key of C identities.

As we invite the full range of our experience, we deepen our capacity to welcome the same from others. In this concluding chapter we will learn how to face the emotional experiences we have tried to avoid for most of our lives. We will discover that the capacity to love with an undefended heart comes from the willingness to turn toward our fear and endure what Saint John called "the dark night of the soul." Only when we have experienced the loss of everything will we discover what cannot be lost.

The Last Defense

Many of the men and women who come to work with us have learned to identify some of their personality strategies, but identifying patterns is not the same as being liberated from them. We may want to change, but perhaps only after we are immersed in the process do we realize the full impact of what is required of us. In order to skirt the fear and pain involved, some try to undertake the passage solely in their minds. But understanding the journey is not the same as taking it.

Elise: Applying the Undefended Approach

Elise approached us after a talk we gave about the ways that couples use money to reinforce their personality defenses. She told us that she and Bill, her partner of fourteen years, keep their money separate. Something about her apparent lack of conscious reflection about this decision caused us to ask her why she had made this choice. Elise explained that she had a long history of never blending finances with primary partners. She enthusiastically volunteered that she had "inherited" this way of doing things from her mother. "My mom came from money and insisted that I keep the 'family money' separate from 'shared funds.'"

Although Elise was aware of the pattern, she failed to see that continuing to follow her mother's directives without making a conscious decision of her own placed limits on her own psychic

structure as well as kept some critical areas unexamined in her relationship. "I like it this way. It feels comfortable," she told us. Sensing
that Elise was using her decision to avoid some emotional discomfort, we asked her what she imagined she would have to confront
were she to consider blending finances with her partner. (At the
same time, we cautioned those listening to our conversation with
Elise that we are not suggesting that everyone in primary partnership should merge their money). Within moments of considering our
question, Elise's face changed, rigidity setting in like a gear locking
into place. Fortunately, she was not a stranger to the introspective
process. With a weak smile, signifying she now understood there
was a "charge" on this issue, she said, "I guess I better look into this
one."

Transformation versus Recognition

Consciously identifying our habits is a clear improvement over
unconsciously living them out. Knowing the ways we try to protect
ourselves gives us greater resilience and flexibility; at the least, we
can begin to take responsibility for our choices. But recognizing a
pattern is different from transforming it. Identifying our armor
leaves the shield intact; we may be less reactive, but we still hide
behind our emotional coat of arms.

In contrast, transforming our defended structure is a process of
dissolving these layers of protection. In the example above, Elise's
investigation into the possibility of combining funds with her partner revealed a host of fears she kept hidden through maintaining
control of her money. Using the process of the vertical drop (see
chapter 6), Elise began her investigation by wondering why she
would trust her heart to someone to whom she wouldn't entrust her
money? Did she value money more than herself and, if so, why?

As she pondered these questions, her distress increased. She
felt mired in confusion and doubt. Her self-image of having it all
together collapsed into old, familiar feelings of being unlovable.
Then, a fresh insight cleared a path to a future direction. "I've experienced very little love in my life. I don't love myself, so why should
anyone else love me? I hold onto my money because it's the only
thing I can hold onto. I can't rely on Bill to stay with me." By challenging the pattern, Elise began another leg of her journey toward

recovering a deeper sense of her own value. Her personal exploration also brought the relationship to its next threshold.

The only way to develop an intimacy that is sustainable is to endure the distress that is evoked when we interrupt our emotional survival strategies. This allows our compensatory identities to crumble—revealing our cracked identities and all the painful feelings attached—and it creates a lasting pathway to our essential self. In the words of Pema Chodron (1997), Abbot of Gampo Abbey in Nova Scotia: "Only to the extent that we expose ourselves over and over to annihilation can that which is indestructible be found in us."

Another way to describe the experience of annihilation is the process of dissolving our defended personality structure. It takes many transits through this process to soften the thickest parts of our armor. And a great joy awaits us: Once we know the way—and gain confidence in its rewards—the journey becomes an adventure that we actively seek out.

Intimate Allies

Exposing ourselves to what we expect will be emotional annihilation is not easy. It means staying with an issue in the presence of our partners when continuing is the hardest thing to do. It means stretching to stay open even if shutting down is our main line of defense. It means speaking about what we are feeling when we are paralyzed with fear. And it means remaining fully present without lashing out when we experience our partners as critical, blaming, or attacking. It even means staying with feeling bad, inadequate, less than, or lacking without doing something to distract ourselves so we can feel better.

In an undefended relationship, instead of bandaging the symptoms, we make a conscious choice to perform the operation that will bring us to and remove the cause of the pain. We are committed to helping each other dissolve—not resolve—our issues. We encourage each other to dive into the truth of our raw inner experience—encountering the core emotional belief that we are unwanted, less than, or flawed—certain that shoring up the personality's defenses is not going to serve either partner in the long term.

While our partner's role is to resist the temptation to fix or distract us from what we are feeling, our role is to endure the resulting discomfort until we unearth the root of our distress. We realize that all our fears and inadequacies are demons we need to encounter on our way back to our open hearts. The undefended path utilizes the inevitable distress and pain that is evoked in relationship to dissolve the lifelong patterns of behavior and reactions that keep us from directly experiencing ourselves and others in an unmediated and unrehearsed way.

Mitch and Patricia: Applying the Undefended Approach

Mitch and Patricia are clients of ours who have been learning to love in an undefended way for several years now. What follows comes from Mitch's journal entries describing an experience of a painful interaction he had with Patricia. In it he moved through the process of dissolving his personality's defenses, which is described in this chapter.

> Patricia was surprised to open the mail and see a confirmation for a speaking engagement I had scheduled for a weekend we had planned to spend together. She was upset. Even though she was entirely responsible in expressing her disappointment—that is, she was not blaming or attacking and began to explore her own reaction instead of purely holding me accountable—I felt myself flush and begin a downward emotional spiral.
>
> I quickly recognized the pit I was tumbling into. I call it my pit of deceit. I felt like a fraud for saying I put our relationship first and then putting work ahead of that value. And I'd been caught. My old personality reflex of reaching for approval and acceptance through work had infiltrated my consciousness and contributed to my making the decision to accept the speaking engagement. I felt deep shame in being witnessed and exposed in this way.
>
> I could readily see the way to solve the *content* of the issue by simply declining the speaking engagement or rescheduling time with Patricia before or after it. That would have put an end to the slippery slope I was sliding down. While a part of me knew that the way "out" is

down, another part of me was being pulled down faster than I would have chosen to go. I was swept away by a tidal wave of old, condemning inner voices: "I always need praise and affirmation from the outside world." "In the end I will fail." And, then the worst one of all, "I will always disappoint the one I love."

I was at once disgusted and heartbroken that these patterns, negative self-concepts and beliefs were still active. In that moment, they were nearly my entire identity. My heart ached so badly I feared I was going to suffer a heart attack. I was vulnerable and naked to the world—certain to be consumed by self-condemnation— and the pull to use my brain to make things better was fierce. "I just made a mistake." "This is no big deal." "Let me make this up to you." "Lighten up." I had to use all my strength not to yield to the multitude of escape routes my mind offered.

When caught in such an avalanche of self-recrimination I often freeze or shut down, so revealing this inner process as it is unfolding is very difficult for me. In this situation, I was able to tell Patricia exactly what was happening inside, although it felt like swimming through molasses to get the words out of my mouth.

While I continued to sink further into my own emotional septic tank—down to the deepest layers of my psychic structure—I was hearing Patricia tumble into her "I am not special" pit. From this place, the world looks capricious and unresponsive to her. What was once a loving universe disappears into a vast, cold emptiness. Brokenhearted, she vacillates between feeling the depth of her disappointment and a despair hardened into "I don't care."

Witnessing Patricia in her own agony felt unbearable to me, yet I knew better than to try to repair what was unfolding. Consciously overwhelmed by my own pain, I was opened by the rawness of her experience and moved to an even deeper layer of my own. My inner witness reminded me that we were not causing each other's suffering. In fact, we could be deeply moved and affected by each other to the point of thinning out another layer of defense.

As we dealt with the many emotional currents between us, I alternated between feeling immobilized and shaken. This was a depth of unhappiness that I had not felt in some time. I wanted to shut down, I wanted to bolt—anything to stop this assault. My mind raced for ways to justify myself. I dragged it back to sit with the heartache.

Even as I persisted and Patricia remained with her sense of hopelessness, there was an aspect of each of us that did not lose sight of the fact we were engaged in a process of revealing flawed self-concepts in a way that would eventually lead to healing and transformation. Because we knew the level of our commitment to this process, we were not afraid that one of us would want to stop or would threaten the relationship rather than continuing on to the next level. It is ironic that this co-commitment was forged in the fires of our personal conviction to do this personal work without the guarantee that the other would do the same.

After several hours of consciously exploring, disclosing, and allowing the feelings to move through us, we ended up feeling purified by the tears and terror of the night's travail. Layers of primitive pain in each of us had been shed, leaving us defenseless yet free from their grasp. The speaking engagement itself had lessened in importance except as the provocation that allowed us to dissolve some old layers of protective covering. The decision to fulfill our commitment to the talk or bow out could go either way, since the outcome no longer held our identities in place. We had arrived at a place of genuine "no preference." We both felt a new and deeper resting place, in ourselves and with each other, feeling lighter yet more substantial.

This last piece of the experience is the true test of determining whether you have come to an undefended place. If, when you return to the *content* of the conflict—that is, the issue that triggered the emotional chain reaction—you continue to feel an emotional charge, your work is not over. Continue to explore and allow the feelings to have more time and space until you are able to discuss the matter in a loving and compassionate manner.

If Mitch and Patricia had each retreated into their compensatory identities, they would have moved increasingly further away from themselves and each other, perhaps even putting the relationship in jeopardy. Instead, by continuing the process as a means of dismantling their defenses, they achieved a deeper intimacy than they had known earlier.

Learning to navigate internal land mines such as these requires a good map of the process as well as all the tools that have been presented thus far. We must build in the expectation that we will lose our way again and again. But with the courage to stay the course when we feel lost, the faith that our essential self is ever-present and the understanding that our struggles are bringing us ever closer to the undefended love we desire, we inevitably reach home again.

The Process of Dissolving

The diagram on the next page provides an overview of the process of dissolving the personality's defenses. In it, we move toward the capacity for deeper connection by releasing our attachment to the layers of our defended personality. Within the domain of personality, represented by the upper triangle of the hourglass image, we must allow our compensatory identities to give way to our cracked identities—a process at once exciting and frightening. As this process continues, we feel increasingly tight, tense, constricted, trapped, or stuck (as we approach the neck of the hourglass). The ensuing fear, despair, or anger keep getting worse. At some point, we enter the Black Hole and experience a flood of feelings from the original experience of separation—alone, empty, annihilated, and disoriented. As we liberate ourselves from this emotional hell-state, we are overtaken by a deep sense of relief and then an expansive, open feeling as we enter a space without limitation. Finally, we come home to the field of undefended intimacy, in the domain of our essential self.

Thus far, we have suggested many ways to use experiences of emotional pain and discomfort to detach from self-limiting identities and cultivate the capacity to be undefended. The following process is the culmination of all that you have learned, mapping the journey taken when you feel the most stuck or upset. Do this process alone

Dissolving Our Defenses

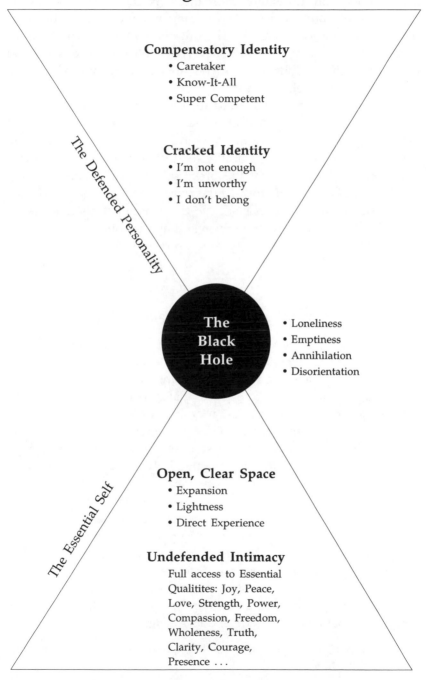

Compensatory Identity
- Caretaker
- Know-It-All
- Super Competent

Cracked Identity
- I'm not enough
- I'm unworthy
- I don't belong

The Defended Personality

The
Black
Hole

- Loneliness
- Emptiness
- Annihilation
- Disorientation

The Essential Self

Open, Clear Space
- Expansion
- Lightness
- Direct Experience

Undefended Intimacy
Full access to Essential
Qualitites: Joy, Peace,
Love, Strength, Power,
Compassion, Freedom,
Wholeness, Truth,
Clarity, Courage,
Presence . . .

or with another. If you choose to do it in the presence of a significant other, understand this is more difficult, so be patient and persevere. Allow for the possibility that you may not make it all the way through the first few times you try, but don't waver in your conviction to go all the way. The intimacy you will experience when you break through the illusion that you are anything but whole and beautiful will be well worth it.

There are roughly five steps to this process of dissolving our defense structure. Regardless of the terror we may feel in the midst of this experience, the more times we traverse this terrain, the more confident we become in our ability to survive the raw feelings that overcome us. Knowing that the process is a natural one, and that each step leads inevitably toward the transformation we most deeply desire, we can relax our resistance to this emotional distress. As we expand our capacity to tolerate the resulting instability and intensity, we recover the essential ability to support ourselves in the face of what we most fear.

Step 1: Move toward Emotional Discomfort

Although our survival-based conditioning has taught us to avoid uncomfortable emotional states, it is imperative that we move toward them if we are committed to living and loving without our personality armor. Any experience that provokes a reaction can serve us in this process: frustration of our needs and wants; a seemingly irreconcilable impasse with our partners; a feeling that we are emotionally trapped; a sense of dissatisfaction with our relationship.

Surprising as it may seem in the early stages of the journey, anxiety, despair, tension, and confusion all indicate a potential for intimate contact. They are what we meet on the way to relating deeply with each other. Just at the point that can lead to the most intimate of meetings, our reflex may be to head for the safety of our compensatory identities. We misinterpret these "negative" states as warning signs of danger, so our first step toward dissolving our defenses is to recognize them as points of entry to deeper connection. The following are some of the most common, although seldom recognized, pathways to undefended loving:

- **Anger**: irritability, impatience, frustration, resentment, hostility, hate

- **Fear**: anxiety, fretting, uneasiness, disturbance, trapped

- **Sadness**: melancholy, loss, grief, depression, loneliness

- **Flatness**: stuck, numb, lifeless, empty, heavy, disinterested

- **Disappointment**: hopelessness, despair, discouragement, disillusionment

- **Discomfort**: tension, overwhelm, constriction

As long as we are not in an abusive relationship, these emotional conditions can actually be gateways to deeper connection, if we move toward them, not away.

As we learn to identify and respond to these possibilities for intimate contact, we discover another powerful pathway to intimacy: The reaction we experience when we cannot tolerate all the love we are receiving—when we reach the upper limit of our capacity for intimacy and emotional intensity. Although we may be accustomed to recoiling from pain, we will see in the example below that contracting from pleasure is also a signal that our defense structures are in effect and that we stand on the edge of breaking through to deeper layers of connection.

Sam and Katie: Applying the Undefended Approach

Sam and Katie are sitting at their favorite cafe in Seattle, reading the Sunday paper and enjoying a break from 92 consecutive days of rain. While Katie is in the restroom, Sam pulls out a couple of airline tickets to Hawaii and puts them down on the travel section of the paper that Katie is reading. When she returns and sees the tickets she attempts to hold her fear in check and pretends to be enthusiastic. (Later, in a therapy session, she discovers she is concerned that spending a week alone with Sam would confirm that they have grown apart, something she doesn't want to face.) While they talk about the trip, Katie begins to wonder out loud if they can afford to leave work right now. As they walk out of the cafe she mentions reading an article about newlyweds on their honeymoon in Hawaii, where the wife was killed by a shark. By the time they get home they are fighting—Sam accusing Katie of being pessimistic and Katie blaming Sam for being too sensitive.

Couples control the intimacy in their relationships—each person knows precisely what to say or do to turn the other off. Mentioning that your wife's mother phoned when the possibility for a sexually intimate evening feels too threatening; choosing to tell your partner that he forgot to set the alarm again just when the conversation is becoming vulnerable; or becoming engaged in a television program when your partner wants to talk about feeling dissatisfied with the relationship—all are perfectly timed to create distance.

So the first step in dissolving our defenses is moving *toward* emotional discomfort—even, and especially, when we feel uncomfortable about the distance or intimacy that is taking place. Only then can we allow our compensatory identities to begin to crumble, revealing our cracked identities.

Step 2: Close All Exits

We all know how it feels when our cracked identities are brought to the surface. It's tormenting, excruciating, scary, and miserable. We get a sinking or churning sensation in the pit of our stomachs; our heads spin; we get hot; we think we're trapped or that we "can't take it anymore." The last thing we want to do is be still. We want to scream at our partners because they seem to be causing this pain in us. We want to get up and go to the store and buy chocolate bars. We want to shut down and shut our partners out. We want to do anything but feel the way we are feeling.

It is exactly at this point that we must *close off our exits* if we are to use our emotional discomfort as a pathway to deeper intimacy. Our exits are the usual ways that we separate from our experience and from our partners. Based on our current set of beliefs—including all the REACT elements discussed in chapter 7 (reciprocity, entitlement, approval, consensus, trustworthiness) and the idea that relationship is a place where we should get our needs met—we make the experience we are having wrong, and we seek to change or override it. We leave ourselves and each other.

Following is a list of the ways we try to get away from whatever is uncomfortable for us. Mentally place a check mark beside the exits you often use when feelings, sensations, and thoughts become too uncomfortable.

- Leave

Leave Physically	*Leave Mentally*
Walk out	Agree to forget about the fight
Get sick	Change the subject
Have accidents	Make mental lists
Feel paralyzed	Intellectualize
Clean the house	Analyze
Exercise	Rationalize
Strike out physically	Count
Fall asleep	Go Blank

  Leave Emotionally
  Become confused
  Shut down
  Get angry
  Talk incessantly
  Experience self-doubt
  Become ambivalent

- Defend
  Lie
  Get indignant
  Become self-righteous
  Justify
  Feel criticized
  Resent

- Indulge an Addiction
  Shop
  Eat
  Watch television
  Use drugs
  Smoke tobacco
  Use alcohol
  Act out sexually
  Relate compulsively
  Act compulsively
  Work
  Engage in fantasy
  Gamble

As you feel yourself moving toward the familiar pit of your particular cracked identity and its negative assessments—"You'll always be lonely"; "No one cares"; "You don't matter"—notice what you do to try to stop yourself from tumbling down into that hole. Then interrupt yourself, take away your means of escape, and let yourself be pulled downward. Of course, you should be in an environment where you can allow yourself to experience this distress. You shouldn't try this while driving or doing something that requires your full attention.

Step 3: Let the Discomfort Overwhelm Your Defenses

Once we close our exits, our distress increases. We may even be tempted to try to hold onto our cracked identity, replaying it in our minds as if it were a mantra: "I am worthless, I am worthless, I am worthless." Do not let your fear, anger, or depression stop your descent. Hanging on to your cracked identity is also a means of escape. You must cling to nothing and let all thoughts cease, surrendering to your experience and allowing it to burn in you, disquiet you, disturb, torment, move, and even disintegrate you.

This is a process of containment in which we neither act on nor suppress our experience—we allow it to be as it is. We permit whatever is happening in us to unfold, without mentally trying to figure out what is happening or why. We can trust that the painful part will pass, and we will experience a deeper sense of our wholeness.

We may lie down and breathe deeply to help us handle the feelings, but we do not take any of our habitual exits. We don't let ourselves believe that this is an experience we should not be having. Instead of identifying with what is happening and concluding that it means something negative about us, we stay present with this uncontrollable experience—without thought, judgment, sentimentality, or drama—until it shifts.

Returning to the example of Sam and Katie mentioned earlier, when Katie reached this step in the process, she felt a deepening sorrow that terrified and upset her. Fortunately, she did not follow her impulse to identify or analyze the sorrow or determine its meaning. (Had she done so, Katie might have decided that she and Sam should get a divorce, that their marriage was a sham, and that she has never loved him—all judgments or conclusions she was in no state to make at this time.) Instead, Katie just let the sorrow deepen. She was miserable and she knew it, and she abided with that misery until she felt the shift.

Distinguishing between Feelings and Reactions

A useful tip at this juncture is to draw the distinction between feelings and reactions. Feelings come in waves: They begin, swell, and subside. They are always in motion. If, at anytime during this process, you feel stuck, you are having a reaction. It may feel like a feeling, but it isn't. When whatever you are experiencing stops flowing, inquire into the reaction until you once again return to feelings.

As the process proceeds, you are likely to come face-to-face with inner demons from your past. You may hear messages that proclaim you are not deserving, not powerful, not respected, not of value, not lovable, or no good. If you feel tortured by these voices, allow yourself to feel the torment, but do not be tempted to follow these thoughts—let them come to the surface and fall away of their own accord. If you fear the pain will shatter your heart, let it break open. Bring to mind the wisdom of Pema Chodron (1997): "When we feel ready to give up, this is the time when healing can be found in the tenderness of the pain itself. . . ." Let yourself face what you have spent your life-energy avoiding. Know the anguish of believing in this mistaken view of yourself; recognize the pain of abandoning yourself when you felt so alone in the past; and open up to the fountains of compassion that spring forth from your heart.

Focus on the Heat

As you abide with this experience, the *heat* of your torment becomes a transformative source of energy, burning off the hardened layers of your personality and fueling your motivation to penetrate the defense structure. It takes a leap of faith to let yourself feel the heat of this transformative fire. Your partner may assist you by being present and witnessing your process, but, in the end, each of us must endure this passage under our own steam. Nobody can do it for us.

Each time you recall whatever initiated this experience of anguish, the burning sensation in your body will return or amplify. Focus on the heat. As your thoughts go wild, accusing or defending, concentrate on what you are feeling. You may suddenly remember a painful memory or event from your past. Whether it is accurate or not, stay with the sensations from this experience. They are leading you back toward that initial loss of contact with your essential self. That is where your liberation begins. Be careful not to react—by dramatizing or denying—because this will reinforce the very structure you are tying to dissolve.

In a sense, this is a bit like yoga. We don't have to tear any muscles in this process. We only have to continue stretching our capacity to tolerate more and more of whatever we experience as unbearable. This is what we must do in any area of our lives when we face and cross our limits. Whether it's public speaking, interviewing for a new job, or moving from closeness to intimacy, we must stretch beyond our prior stage of comfort.

We once asked a well-known athlete who was training for a marathon if professional runners ever get to the point where there is no physical discomfort, where they no longer have to experience intense resistance at some point in the run. She answered: "At this point in my career I look for signs of physical discontent and invite them in. That way I know that my body is doing what it needs to do to get me through the next challenge. Nowadays, I get scared if I *don't* feel uncomfortable." The same is true in cultivating undefended intimacy. If we don't feel the emotional stretch as we go beyond our limits, we may be unconsciously replaying a familiar pattern. This is not to say that our relationships become focused on pain; it's rather that we are not free until we are able to welcome the full spectrum of feelings.

Remember, fear and pain cause us to contract, and kindness neutralizes that contraction, allowing us to stay open. The attitude of compassion is our guide, helping us penetrate the layers of defense and suffering to reach the precious gold of essence. It is the sacred escort to the truth of ourselves. When we resist the usual escape strategies, we discover that our present suffering ushers us back to our original experience of loss when we separated from our intrinsic wholeness. This is a critical point in the process.

Step 4: Enter the Black Hole

As our habitual self-images and ways of relating to others begin to collapse and fragment, we enter the "Black Hole." This is the transition point between the final layer of personality and the threshold of the essential domain, a place where we have lost contact with both our compensatory and cracked identities. It feels like an endless chasm we will never survive—the end of the road, death, annihilation, or the big nothing. Indeed, in terms of our defense structures, that's what it is. At this point, when our personality's fortress walls are dismantled and ineffectual, we discover the nightmare we have been trying to flee.

All spiritual traditions eventually address that, in the end, it is not pain that people are afraid of, it is emptiness. Emptiness is what we loathe and hate the most. In fact, we would rather stay in deficiency than experience this. We'd rather hate ourselves than be nothing.

Clients have described this experience as "nonconnection to anything," the "valley of death," "that black, empty nothing-and-nowhere place," or "hell." They report feeling disoriented, empty, alone, and hollow. They fear they may go crazy. Their bodies feel cold (although some report feeling outrageously hot) with temporary sensations of nausea or dizziness.

It can be terrifying, and we seldom feel we have the tolerance to bear the distress; however, we must remember that endurance is possible. With each pass through the black hole we become more resilient and trusting that the experience will indeed shift. If we do not prematurely stop the process, we feel a tremendous sense of release on the other side of it.

The threshold of the Black Hole is a point of critical choice. In response to our fears, the defended personality wants to head for a safe harbor to ride out the storm. However, the approach that produces intimacy and leads us to our essential self is to turn, like a boat in a winter squall, and head into the waves. We must confront the inner emptiness and loneliness that rise up from our deepest sense of deficiency. In the Black Hole, we are face-to-face with our initial experience of separation, frozen in time, frozen in us—only now we have the adult capacity to endure the experience consciously. As we stop relying on external supports, we discover the fathomless reservoir of our essential self. Now we can provide for ourselves the support that was not available to us years ago. In this inner void we need the same three supports we spoke of in chapter 3: emotional presence, reassurance, and mirroring.

Emotional Presence

We must open our hearts and stay with our inner experience, not try to distract, repress, deny, or move away from what we are feeling in any way. Our unwavering commitment must be to remain present to ourselves, fully engaged with what we are experiencing, and, if possible, love ourselves despite the pull to self-judge.

In this process, it can be helpful to return to the practice described in an earlier chapter where you imagine yourself as a young boy or girl (perhaps at the age of three or four) going through similar emotional distress. How would you relate to this young child? How could you express your love and support? What would you want to communicate to him or her? Perhaps you would touch his hand to let him know you were there for him. Or, you might hold her so she knows she won't be left alone. You might want to tell him that everything is going to be okay. Now, do this for yourself in the midst of your distress.

Reassurance

Instead of interpreting it as a life sentence, we need to remember that the experience of being in the Black Hole, like all other experiences, has a beginning, a middle, and an end. We are not really going to die or go crazy, even though we fear that we will. We must stretch to tolerate it, not pull away from it. We must embrace the waves of feelings fully until they subside of their own accord. Knowing that they will pass helps us to bear our unhappiness.

Mirroring

When we are in the Black Hole, the level of contact with our essential self will be out of the reach of our consciousness. We need to have faith and explicitly remind ourselves that we are indeed complete, good, strong, and valuable. We must remember that our persistence will bring us home to our intrinsically whole and pure nature, where we can once again be undefended and reside permanently in love.

Shifting to Release

The inner friction, anxiety, and tension we experience when we allow ourselves to endure the Black Hole wears down the wall between the outer domain of personality and the inner domain of essence. Satprem (1993), chronicler of Sri Aurobindo's teachings, describes it this way: "The seeker will feel this wall slowly losing its consistency; he will experience a kind of change in the texture of his being, as if he were becoming lighter, more porous. . . ."

An amazing shift occurs. The terror releases, the heat cools, and this deeply uncomfortable experience eases. The darkness becomes an almost luminous blackness that paradoxically feels light-giving, inviting, and clear. The feeling that we are disappearing or breaking up into a thousand pieces recedes into an abiding sense of stillness, freedom, and deep connection. Instead of feeling deficient, empty, and alone, we feel a sense of open space, expansive and light. We feel complete, not needing anything to be other than it is. One habitual ground of being has been replaced by another in which we are at ease exactly as we are. We are at peace. We are peace itself.

At this point in the process we have suspended thought entirely. Instead of observing what is happening, we are directly experiencing it. All of us, at one time or another, have known what it is to be at one with pure experience. Perhaps through sports, music, nature, or a sexual experience we have "lost ourselves" by letting go of the observer. It is the instant when there is no longer an "us" and an "other"; there is only the experience itself. In music, it is the moment when the audience and the musicians disappear and only listening remains.

When the defended personality dissolves, what is left is *direct experience*. The open space gives way to essence, and we feel full, rich, and substantial. This is the gateway to relating in a fresh way. We are present—right here, right now—unbuffered by the past and unburdened by the future. In this sense, we lose ourselves and find ourselves—we lose what we no longer need and find what has never been lost.

Learning to pass through the Black Hole is like learning to successfully mine for gold. The gold, our lost qualities of essence, is hidden down a deep dark mine shaft that caved in many years ago. Every time we enter that dark tunnel, we feel fear. The more trips we take, the better we get at navigating the hazardous stretch of the Black Hole. This is where we recover our treasure, the qualities of our essential self, buried so long ago. We come to relationship, then, truly naked, undefended, and fully available.

Step 5: Articulating Our Experience in the Absence of a Defended Personality

Describing our experience on the other side of the Black Hole is a crucial step as we deepen the connection with our essence and create a level of undefended intimacy that can be sustained. To do this we must draw on senses that are just beginning to develop. It is like entering a darkened room and allowing our eyes to get used to the darkness. We must learn to see, hear, smell, and taste this new open space—it feels unknown, but very alive and fresh.

It takes time, courage, and strength to struggle with perceiving and articulating this experience. The more we step out of the predetermined grooves of personality, the more we must forge a new vocabulary that can expand to describe what is revealed. We begin to seek words that before we may have felt belonged only to lyricists, poets, and spiritualists. We speak of ourselves as solid, luminous, clear, joyful, light, soft, ripe, purified, content, radiant, divine, magnificent, and mysterious.

In the process of searching for new ways of expressing ourselves, we learn to let go of using personality as our reference point. We respond spontaneously to each situation. When asked to dance, instead of declining because we "don't dance" we get up and do whatever comes naturally. When we feel sad, we don't "buck up" because big boys don't cry. Instead, we openly shed the tears that are there and welcome the presence and possibly the comfort of those witnessing us. We look for new emotional pathways to experience intimacy instead of playing old, habitual roles of waiting to be pursued or chasing after to produce the energy to connect.

We become accustomed to doing whatever we can to relate essentially, rather than depending on favorable external circumstances (such as falling in love, starting a new work project, or buying a new home) to produce the result for us. We learn to live and relate from the essence we are now allowing to shine through.

When these five steps to the dissolving process are taken on your own, or in a spiritual or therapeutic environment, they wear down, loosen, and melt the armor of the defended personality. When they are taken in the presence of a significant other, their by-product is undefended intimacy. We do not cultivate intimacy through wrestling our partners to the mat, but through struggling with ourselves on each issue. In this way, we develop the internal support that replaces our dependency on external sources. This allows us to increase our capacity for the upper limits of joy and the lower limits of emotional torment. As our tolerance for difficult emotions increases, so does our capacity to experience the expansive ones.

Taking the Journey

Must we go through this entire process every time we face an impasse, incompatibility, or issue in our relationships? We can work on many levels to peel back and subsequently dissolve our defended personalities. Some are more intense than others; however, only through successfully navigating the Black Hole do we gain an unshakable conviction in our essential self.

Cynthia: Applying the Undefended Approach

Cynthia, a woman in her mid-forties, used this process to deal with a painful event in her relationship. She came to one of our retreats because her partner, Justin, had had an affair. When she began the week, she held the position that he was wrong and had betrayed her trust, which she feared could never be recovered. In an opening group process she focused her attention and attacks on Justin's behavior, seeing herself as the victim and feeling self-righteous and outraged.

At first, Cynthia was more than a little resistant to looking at any way that she might have contributed to creating an environment that would lead to a betrayal of that kind. She did admit that in her prior relationships, she had encountered similar issues of loyalty and betrayal. She began to realize that even if she were to end her current relationship, she might once again face the same pattern. This enabled her to suspend her accusations long enough to turn her attention inward.

Cynthia began by wondering if the affair might be related to something that neither she nor Justin had been able to face directly. Perhaps only something this big could get them to look at it. For her part, this meant acknowledging an uncomfortable feeling that she was "not enough." It probably also accounted for the reason she hadn't been available to hear the truth about Justin's pain. She identified places where she had withdrawn from him in subtle and not so subtle ways. She had been critical and demeaning of him as a means of pushing him away so she would not have to face vulnerable and raw places in herself. Although these behaviors had not "caused" the affair, Cynthia could choose to use the affair as an opportunity to examine herself and her relationship.

The process of arriving at these insights was slow and arduous. Many times along the way she attempted to exit. As we facilitated her process, a fellow workshop member recorded a list of the layers Cynthia encountered before she could drop into the Black Hole:

- Self-criticism

- Embarrassment

- Feeling overwhelmed

- Going blank

- Physical discomfort

- Jokes

- Mind racing to different, unrelated subjects

- I can't do this

At each point that she could have backed off from the inquiry, Cynthia persevered, giving herself the opportunity to feel the pain and periodically allowing it to break her heart open. Guided away from familiar escape routes, she held her own feet to the transformative fire—resisting the temptation to blame, shut down, or distract herself from the discomfort—and her courage moved us all.

As Cynthia entered the Black Hole, it was clear that she was marshaling all of her willpower to stay there. "I feel all alone. It's black, cold, and deep in here. I'm free falling and there's nothing there to hold me. I feel sick in my stomach—like it's tied up in a knot."

A little while later, just as we could see Cynthia begin to relax, she tensed again and said, "I've lost it." We quickly responded, "You haven't lost it. The experience has shifted. Describe it." Cynthia had mistaken the disappearance of her turmoil to mean she had shut down or interrupted the process. This can be a common misperception as we emerge on the other side of the Black Hole. Encouraged to articulate instead of evaluate what she was experiencing, she realized a new place had opened inside of her, one that was unfamiliar and wonderful.

Initially clients are hesitant to describe this experience. It feels too fresh, too wonderful, too amazing. When encouraged, they feel shy about using the words that come to mind, such as "delicious," "exquisite," "tender," and "lovely." These expressions feel unfamiliar, lyrical, and rhapsodic, resulting in self-consciousness. Their dilemma is that they do not know themselves as poets, yet they cannot describe their experience without waxing poetic.

This was true of Cynthia, who needed a lot of encouragement to tell us what she was feeling. "I feel free, floating, like on a river. It's more gray now, not black, like a mist rising off a pond in the morning. It's peaceful. It's a gentle landing, almost a cradling, rocking me back and forth." As Cynthia spoke, some tears welled up and an early memory, long buried, rose in her consciousness. She recalled how she would sit in her mother's lap in an alcove in the kitchen, early in the morning. Her mother would rock back and forth, holding her and watching the birds outside on the pond beside the house. "It was our special time together. We'd talk and talk. My heart felt completely open and safe."

This marked one passage through the Black Hole for Cynthia. Throughout the retreat, she used the distress over the affair to initiate this inner dissolving, holding to her resolve to reach the deepest layers of truth by openly confronting herself. Soon the exhilaration from connecting with the depth of her being began to outweigh the discomfort of the experience. Cynthia felt tremendous relief and release with each new level of realization. This repeated intimate experience—of opening, struggling, and letting go—brought about an increasing certainty that she could indeed traverse this difficult passage to transformation.

By the closing ceremony for the retreat, Cynthia had not only stopped blaming her partner and defending herself, she was ready to respond with compassion to the circumstances of Justin's affair. Taking responsibility for not addressing signs of his increasing distress in the course of their relationship, she no longer hoped the situation would just go away. She let the pain guide her to the next threshold with her partner. As she allowed her defenses to crumble, taking her to emotional places she had avoided her entire life, Cynthia gained access to the inner resources she needed to face this challenge. She felt ready to "do the work"—to use the affair to strengthen, not destroy, her relationship, which she still valued and wished to continue.

What she reported to the other members of the workshop in the closing circle the final weekend is an eloquent teaching, valuable for all of us: "I don't want to separate from Justin. I want to separate from the ways we have related with one another. I want to separate from the system he and I have developed together that is no longer serving either one of us."

When we respond from an undefended heart, we feel at one with everything, completely free. In Cynthia's words, "When I'm in this place I am no longer reacting to what is happening, and I am no longer ignoring what is happening." We are entirely present to our life—centered in our truth—and responding from our deepest nature.

Cynthia endured a painful passage in her relationship by using her emotional distress to know a larger truth. Having survived this nightmare, she recognized resources inside her that she never knew she had. She sharpened her capacity to tolerate discomfort, anxiety, and emotional pain. She realized that relationship is a personal journey of recovery and discovery in which one feels stretched, broken, rattled, and shattered. In this dismantling of her personality defenses, she released some of her safety-and-control armor and discovered the power of undefended relating. This was a new and indestructible kind of safety. She now knew how to come to relationship undefended and unrehearsed.

Postponement: The Toughest Challenge to the Quest

One of the challenges we face in cultivating intimacy is the habit of postponing the work we need to do on ourselves. In part, this habit comes from the illusion that we have endless time. We don't. We are all here for a limited time. As one client good-naturedly told his fiancée after she delayed their wedding plans a second time, "You better act soon, because I'm a limited-time offer."

When all of your accomplishments are examined at the end of your lifetime, by which ones will you be most deeply moved? What do you imagine will fill your heart with joy when you are ninety-two years old, reflecting on your life? What will leave an inward smile lingering as you review who you have become after all these years?

In our work with couples and individuals, the answers to these questions always include how well we have loved, how wholeheartedly we have given of ourselves, what personal meaning and power we have invested in our journey, and the ways in which we have stretched beyond the identity we thought we had to meet our partners in an undefended way.

Despite the evidence that remembering our essential self provides the only permanent satisfaction, the temptation to sleepwalk through life, until we hit a wall that forces us to wake up, is immense. For this reason, many doubt they can meet the challenge of undefended love.

Postponement is the belief that we are not ready or strong enough to do something, coupled with the fear of the further disappointment if we try and fail. In this way, postponement is a numbing agent. By putting off struggling with the question of what we essentially desire, by putting off witnessing our behavior or challenging our thoughts and feelings, we put *ourselves* off until some later time that we secretly hope will never come. But Gangaji (1993b) reminds us: "Don't miss this opportunity—who knows when it will come again? This lifetime, this year, this moment you have the absolute capacity to know who you are."

Every emotional state can be an entry point to an intimate experience of ourselves and another if we can learn to recognize it and make use of it. All of our reactions, behaviors, thoughts, and feelings can serve this purpose, as can all of the places where we feel stuck, blocked, or stopped in our tracks. You begin where you are. If your habit is to postpone, then that is your entry point to the intimacy you seek; it just looks a little different from what you might have expected.

Something motivates the habit of postponing, and this needs to be recognized. Chances are you will discover emotional pain, fear, or anger based in some unresolved past issue. Bring that recognition with you, enter the quest through this gateway, and you will discover that you can use even the desire to postpone to create a deeper experience of yourself and another. In the end, the level of peace, love, and pleasure we are capable of enjoying corresponds to the depth of emotional pain we can tolerate. It is our depth that defines the fullness and intensity of intimacy we can experience with another. To live an undefended life, we must love all that is—what we consider desirable and undesirable, good and bad, natural and unnatural—and know it to be part of who we are. As we rest in this radiance, intoxicated at times, full and complete, our love becomes like an eternal natural spring.

The Liberation of Undefended Love

Namaste

I honor the place within you where
the entire universe resides.

I honor the place within you of love and light,
of peace and truth.

I honor the place within you where,
when you are in that place in you
and I am in that place in me,
there is only one of us.

—Anonymous

Once we have experienced undefended intimacy enough times to know that it exceeds all expectations for what is possible between two people, we are willing to suffer whatever distress and emotional pain is necessary to permanently abide there. At this point in the journey, something occurs which Marlena and I simply, but reverently, refer to as *the flip*.

The flip happens when the pain of not expressing the full spectrum of our essential qualities exceeds our fear of doing so. It is the point at which our anguish over not loving ourselves and each other from our deepest core exceeds the fear of not protecting ourselves.

As we have seen, this does not mean that our fears and reactions disappear. It simply means that we are willing to struggle with them in the service of creating a more meaningful and openhearted experience of ourselves and our partners.

Paradoxically, beyond the flip everything changes, and nothing changes. In other words, our external circumstances may or may not change, but how we relate to them and the use we make of them is dramatically different. This is a revolutionary transition in our personal and relationship development that can occur suddenly or over time. You will know when it happens because you will feel the shift in the very deepest part of you. You will be moved to say, "I will allow what I am experiencing and inquire into it," even if your knees are shaking and your will feels small.

After the flip, the world as we have known it to be—through the lens of our defended personalities—turns upside down. Experiences and feelings that used to be seen as obstacles are now viewed as entry points to experiencing deeper levels of connection, with ourselves and with others. We no longer view those times when we experience our relationship as "not working" as portending its end and heralding the time to look elsewhere. We respond, instead, by looking for the places within us in which we have outgrown our current context, exploring areas where we need to be stretched, dismantled, and reformed. We recognize our problems and dissatisfactions as wake-up calls pointing out our readiness to come into deeper relationship with some lost aspect of our beings. The more rooted a couple is in essence-centered relating, the more deeply the two welcome the inevitable earthquakes beneath and between them, for these are opportunities to carve deeper canyons of love than they have achieved thus far.

Our communication, too, changes dramatically with the advent of the flip. The old, automatic response of seeing each other as "the problem" is replaced with a new reflex of inquiring into the response that is evoked in us. Instead of maintaining an outward focus—on our partners—we are inwardly focused on unraveling the source of our reaction.

Although couples committed to undefended love don't really complain or argue, this does not mean they don't experience tension or that their discussions lack intensity. The difference is that their energy does not go outward in blaming and attacking, nor do they withdraw. They engage and participate fully with their own inner conflicts without assigning them to anyone else. They seek to recognize that the presence of the other in their lives serves an invaluable purpose: to increase the internal pressure each experiences, which, in turn, provides both with the energy needed to see and dissolve all layers of defense.

To one who has not experienced the flip, this description of relationship might seem impersonal, but nothing can be further from the truth. It is highly interpersonal and involved, but not conflictual. When triggered, instead of interacting on the level of "You did this and I did that," each partner holds four separate realities concurrently:

1. They stay fully present to their own emotional pain and the confusion or discomfort that is evoked.

2. They stay fully present to the other's emotional pain and its unfolding process, remaining receptive to the experience in an empathic, available, and emotionally nonreactive way.

3. They stay fully present to the deepest experience of their essential selves that they can access.

4. In their consciousness, they hold the most unobstructed view of the deepest core of the other.

This process is intensely personal, requiring the ability to maintain direct contact with ourselves and undefended contact with each other. A client of ours, Chelsie, after striving to maintain this level of truth during a particularly challenging evening with her partner, told us: "After talking with Ted all night I feel as if we made love. I feel such deep gratitude for the way he made room for primitive and unformed energies in me to come out. This morning there is not even a membrane left to cover my heart."

New and Undefended Choices

To receive and to offer unconditional love, we must become undefended and unconditioned lovers. Having realized the depths to which our personality strategies have kept us isolated and empty, we begin to make new choices. We search for the truth of our direct experience instead of reenacting our old defensive strategies. When we experience emotional distance in our relationships, we look for the ways we have separated from ourselves reflected in the disconnection from our partners. When we feel hostile, we recognize we are trying to feel powerful and allow ourselves to be overwhelmed by the truth of our powerlessness. When we feel alone, we resist the temptation to distract ourselves or to connect on superficial levels. Instead, we use our experience as an opportunity to discover the fullness of "alone," and its call to deepen our connection with the intrinsic qualities of our essential self.

Wearing our personalities lightly, we experience everything more directly, more profoundly, and more intensely. The love, joy, and pleasure are felt more and enjoyed more. But we are also vulnerable to feeling our emotional pain, discomfort, tension, anxiety, and losses more acutely. We can only experience undefended intimacy on the raw edge of life, where we resurface from our protected hiding place and come into direct contact with ourselves and our partners.

A delightful client with whom we worked for several years described it this way: "Something happened as a result of grappling with all of these issues; a reconciliation with and appreciation of my humanness. Now I'm celebrating the very limitations and imperfections that before were the source of major suffering. My relationship feels so rich and full of texture, it makes 'perfection' look very sterile."

Instead of trying to maintain a sense of harmony by limiting who we are, we embrace our partners as intimate allies. We invite them to challenge us and point out where we have fallen asleep. Through this process, our personality is transformed into a vehicle for awakening instead of a fortress of unconsciousness. After resurfacing from a deep passage of exploration with his wife, a good friend of ours lovingly remarked: "She is a constant beacon. In the presence of her bright light I see where my shadow falls, and I cannot go to sleep." He can say this because, over the years, he has come to value his wife's challenges to his personality structure. "She helps me see where I am recycling old patterns. Through my own reactions I can see the many places where I have lost access to my sense of balance and well-being. The mirror she holds up to me shows me the belief systems that obstruct my full potential to love."

Deepening Relationships with Others and Ourselves

Initially, we can and often will feel uncomfortable as the illusions of control and safety are scraped away. Over time, as we learn to stop struggling and let go into the experience, the contact is less harsh. Slowly, the hardened layers of our defense system are peeled away and dissolved, and the walls between us become ever thinner. As we become more exposed, we become more illuminated in the glow of our essential self and revel in the glow of our partner's beauty.

We become less attached to outcome and more invested in deepening our experience of the present. Our loving finds a new depth, one that is both personal and nonpersonal. We take residence in a field of love, flexible to respond as appropriate, spontaneous and alive to the movements within and between us. No longer distracted by the din of our thoughts, feelings, and sensations, we experience ourselves as large enough to encompass all of reality—congruent and incongruent—in its fullness and complexity.

As we proceed further along the intimate path outlined in these pages we come to the final satisfaction of the dual yearning of the human heart. We realize that relationship is not where we lose ourselves—rather it is the place where we meet ourselves and know the "other" to be ourselves. In the words of the thirteenth-century mystic and poet Rumi, "The minute I heard my first love story I went looking for you, not knowing how blind that was. Lovers don't finally meet somewhere. They are in each other all along" (Rumi 1997).

As you travel further along the path of undefended intimacy, you will discover that the relationship journey is not about two people becoming one. It is about realizing that we are all one vast, loving, universal heart.

Bibliography

Almaas, A. H. 1987. *Diamond Heart, Book One: Elements of the Real in Man*. Berkeley, California: Diamond Books.

Chodron, Pema. 1997. *When Things Fall Apart*. Boston: Shambala.

de Mille, Agnes. 1991. *Martha: The Life and Work of Martha Graham*. New York: Random House.

Frankl, Viktor. 1984. *Man's Search for Meaning*. New York: Touchstone, Simon & Schuster.

Gangaji. 1993a. Audio tape of "Satsang with Gangaji" in Boulder, Colo. Pacific Center Press, The Gangaji Foundation: Kula, Hawaii. August 9.

Gangaji. 1993b. Audio tape of "Satsang with Gangaji" in Santa Fe. Pacific Center Press, The Gangaji Foundation: Kula, Hawaii. October 10.

Gurdjieff, G. I. 1973. *Views from the Real World*. New York: E.P. Dutton.

Hallmark Hall of Fame Productions Inc., in association with Sofronski Productions. 1996. *Harvest of Fire*.

Klein, Jean. 1984. *The Ease of Being*. Durham, N.C.: The Acorn Press.

Kornfield, Jack. 1993. *A Path with Heart*. New York: Bantam Books.

Levine, Stephen and Ondrea. 1984. *Embracing the Beloved*. New York: Doubleday.

Lynch/Frost Productions, Inc., in association with Propoganda Films in association with Worldvision Enterprises, Inc. 1989. "Fire Walk With Me," episode of *Twin Peaks*.

Mahler, Margaret. 1975. *The Psychological Birth of the Human Infant.* New York: Basic Books.

Poonji, H. W. L. 1992. *Wake Up and Roar, Volume 1.* Kula, Maui, Hawaii: Pacific Center Publishing.

Rilke, Ranier Maria. 1954. *Letters to a Young Poet.* New York: W. W. Norton.

Rumi. 1997. *The Essential Rumi.* Translations by Coleman Barks, with John Moyne. New Jersey: Castlebooks.

Satprem. 1993. *Sri Aurobindo on the Adventure of Consciousness.* Paris: Institut de Recherches Evolutives.

Schnarch, David. 1991. *Constructing the Sexual Crucible.* New York: W. W. Norton.

Seng-can. 1999. The *Xin-xin-ming* (Faith-Mind Maxim) from *Three Chan Classics,* trans.Yoshida Osamu. Berkeley, California: Numata Center for Buddhist Translation and Research.

Shikibu, Izumi. 1990. "Watching the Moon," from *The Ink Dark Moon: Love Poems,* trans. Jane Hirschfield with Mariko Aratani. New York: Vintage Books.

Sogyal Rinpoche. 1992. *The Tibetan Book of Living and Dying.* New York: HarperCollins.

Welwood, Jennifer. 1998. *Poems for the Path.* Mill Valley, California: Copyright by Jennifer Welwood.

Contact Us

 Jett Psaris and Marlena S. Lyons would like to hear from you about your experience loving in an undefended way. Please write to them by Earthmail at the address below or contact them through their Web site:

www.Undefendedlove.com.

Jett and Marlena offer workshops and retreats based on the principles and practices presented in this book. These programs are appropriate for couples, individuals, health professionals, and others interested in emotionally intimate partnerships, self-realization, and personal development. If you wish to receive information about their programs please write to them at the address below, phone, or send an e-mail. Details will be sent to you upon request.

Jett Psaris and Marlena S. Lyons
The Conscious Living Center
6357 Westover Drive
Oakland, CA 94611
Tel: 510-482-9998
Fax: 510-482-9992
Web site: http://www.Undefendedlove.com

Jett Psaris, Ph.D., and Marlena Lyons, Ph.D., are cofounders of the Conscious Living Center, a counseling and workshop center in the San Francisco Bay Area. They have been leading seminars and retreats that guide couples and individuals to cultivate the capacity for undefended love—with oneself as well as with others—since 1990. Marlena has been in private practice specializing in relationship issues since 1979. Jett came to the field of psycho-spiritual work in 1988, after a decade in business as an executive in several high-profile companies.

Through their work together, they have gone beyond researching the reasons why people have failed to create exceptional relationships and have developed a unique approach to accelerate personal and relationship development to allow individuals to connect with themselves and each other in an undefended and open way.

More New Harbinger Titles

WHY ARE WE STILL FIGHTING?
How to End Your Schema Wars and Start Connecting with the People You Love

Explains how our mental models about the world can short-circuit our relationships and offers strategies for effective long-term change.
Item FIGH $15.95

WOMEN'S SEXUALITIES
Generations of Women Share Intimate Secrets of Sexual Self-Acceptance

Startling new data from a breakthrough survey helps readers understand the conditions that lead women to positive sexual growth and self-acceptance.
Item WOSE $15.95

SEX SMART
How Your Childhood Shaped Your Sexual Life and What to Do About It

Detailed self-tests and exercises help your understand your sexual issues and suggest strategies for counteracting troublesome emotional patterns learned long ago.
Item SESM $16.95

INFIDELITY
A Survival Guide

Step-by-step guidance shows how to cope with the emotional impact of an affair and either choose to break up or begin to rebuild.
Item INFI Paperback $14.95

THE POWER OF TWO

Learn strategies for making decisions together, recovering after upsets, and converting difficulties into opportunities for growth.
Item PWR Paperback $15.95

Call **toll-free 1-800-748-6273** to order. Have your Visa or Master-card number ready. Or send a check for the titles you want to New Harbinger Publications, 5674 Shattuck Avenue, Oakland, CA 94609. Include $4.50 for the first book and 75¢ for each additional book to cover shipping and handling. (California residents please include appropriate sales tax.) Allow four to six weeks for delivery.

Prices subject to change without notice.

Some Other
New Harbinger Titles

The Well-Ordered Office, Item 3856 $13.95

Talk to Me, Item 3317 $12.95

Romantic Intelligence, Item 3309 $15.95

Transformational Divorce, Item 3414 $13.95

The Rape Recovery Handbook, Item 3376 $15.95

Eating Mindfully, Item 3503 $13.95

Sex Talk, Item 2868 $12.95

Everyday Adventures for the Soul, Item 2981 $11.95

A Woman's Addiction Workbook, Item 2973 $18.95

The Daughter-In-Law's Survival Guide, Item 2817 $12.95

PMDD, Item 2833 $13.95

The Vulvodynia Survival Guide, Item 2914 $15.95

Love Tune-Ups, Item 2744 $10.95

The Deepest Blue, Item 2531 $13.95

The 50 Best Ways to Simplify Your Life, Item 2558 $11.95

Brave New You, Item 2590 $13.95

Loving Your Teenage Daughter, Item 2620 $14.95

The Hidden Feelings of Motherhood, Item 2485 $14.95

The Woman's Book of Sleep, Item 2418 $14.95

Pregnancy Stories, Item 2361 $14.95

The Women's Guide to Total Self-Esteem, Item 2418 $13.95

Thinking Pregnant, Item 2302 $13.95

The Conscious Bride, Item 2132 $12.95

Juicy Tomatoes, Item 2175 $13.95

Call **toll free, 1-800-748-6273,** or log on to our online bookstore at **www.newharbinger.com** to order. Have your Visa or Mastercard number ready. Or send a check for the titles you want to New Harbinger Publications, Inc., 5674 Shattuck Ave., Oakland, CA 94609. Include $4.50 for the first book and 75¢ for each additional book, to cover shipping and handling. (California residents please include appropriate sales tax.) Allow two to five weeks for delivery.

Prices subject to change without notice.